Outrageous
Facts About
Murders,
Maniacs,
and Mayhem

TOTALLY
TERRIFYING
TRUE CRIME
TRIVIA

BRIAN BOONE

CASTLE POINT
BOOKS

www.castlepointbooks.com

The Castle Point Books trademark is owned by Castle Point Publishing, LLC.
Castle Point books are published and distributed by St. Martin's Publishing Group.

ISBN 978-1-250-28722-9 (trade paperback)
ISBN 978-1-250-28736-6 (ebook)

Cover and interior design by Joanna Williams

Our books may be purchased in bulk for promotional, educational, or business use.
Please contact your local bookseller or the Macmillan Corporate and
Premium Sales Department at 1-800-221-7945, extension 5442,
or by email at MacmillanSpecialMarkets@macmillan.com.

First Edition: 2023

10 9 8 7 6 5 4 3 2

CONTENTS

ꟾNTRODUCTION

It's a truth, albeit a dark one, that human beings are capable of committing heinous acts of violence against one another—murder, mass eradication, kidnapping, assault, and attacks driven by a fit of rage, passion, or even insanity.

Because of how rare and shocking these deathly events are, we can't help but be curious, even obsessed, with the details of a criminal act. The true crime aficionado is hungry for knowledge and harbors a bottomless fascination with books, movies, documentaries, and podcasts about actual murders, the murderers' motivations, and the investigations that bring (or don't bring) perpetrators to justice. Maybe if we look closely enough, and examine all the little details and clues under a magnifying glass, we can make sense of the horror, and be ready to spot a killer or solve a murder if we ever have the chance.

Totally Terrifying True Crime Trivia is a creepy compendium of captivatingly dark and deeply interesting reveals about true crimes. Take a daring tour inside and find fascinating nuggets of information that might as well have been lifted straight from the police files. By the end of this book, you'll be eerily familiar with some of the most notorious and frightening criminals in history, their nefarious acts, and the fate that befell them.

CHAPTER 1

Murder Most Foul

The most bizarre, horrifying,
and surprising tales of murder
history has to offer.

John Walsh, creator and host of *America's Most Wanted*, had a six-year-old son who was abducted and murdered.

While his mother looked at lamps at a Sears in July 1981, Adam Walsh went to check out the Atari games. Some teens were playing, got into a fight about whose turn it was, and store security threw everybody out, including Adam. After ninety minutes of fruitless searching in and around the store for Adam, Revé Walsh contacted police. Two weeks later, the severed head of Adam Walsh was found in a drainage canal 130 miles away. Two years later, serial killer Ottis Toole, in prison for a different murder, confessed to Walsh's murder, which he later recanted. Authorities still determined Toole to be responsible, and the case was closed. The tragedy inspired Adam's father, John, to create a show that could bring justice and closure to other families.

Snuff films are an urban legend.

"Snuff films," videotaped records of the murder of a human being, factor prominently into the plots of many unsettling movies, but they aren't real. No law enforcement agency in the U.S., Europe, or Asia has ever discovered one. Their existence is an urban legend, set off in the early 1970s, when filmmaker Ed Sanders claimed in the Charles Manson documentary *The Family* that the murder cult had used Super-8 cameras to make "brutality films." No such tapes ever surfaced.

Kathleen Peterson may have died as the result of an owl attack.

The popular true crime documentary *The Staircase* made it seem like Michael Peterson had killed his wife, Kathleen, in 2001 by pushing her down a flight of stairs. Peterson was convicted but later released on a technical error by the prosecution, leading his attorney to investigate the possible real killer: a barred owl. Native to the Petersons' hometown in coastal North Carolina, barred owls are known to attack humans unprovoked. Kathleen Peterson's head bore talon marks, and owl feathers were discovered on her body.

An exonerated murderer met the real perpetrator of the crimes he didn't commit in prison.

Kirk Bloodsworth was found guilty for the 1984 murder of a nine-year-old Maryland girl, despite a lack of compelling physical evidence and a solid alibi. The conviction was overturned, but Bloodsworth was convicted once more. In 1992, he was exonerated by DNA evidence and finally cleared and released. In 2002, the real murderer in the case was found: Kimberly Shay Ruffer, in prison for another crime. Bloodsworth knew the man— they'd been friends in prison, their sentences overlapping. They traded library books.

The *Amityville Horror* was inspired by a real-life murder house.

The horror movie franchise *The Amityville Horror* is based on a book that recounts the allegedly true story of George and Kathy Lutz, who moved into a house in Amityville, New York, where Ronald DeFeo murdered his parents and four siblings while they slept in 1974. They moved out after a month, claiming to be tormented by evil spirits, the same ones that must have directed DeFeo to kill his family. After the release of *The Amityville Horror* book, DeFeo's attorney, William Weber, sued the Lutzes for breach of contract after cutting him out of the publishing deal. Weber revealed that he and the Lutzes had gotten drunk one night and invented the entire haunted house story.

A high-ranking military officer used jogging as a cover for underwear theft and murder.

Canadian Armed Forces colonel David Williams claimed he was going on daily runs in 2007, but he was really breaking into neighbors' homes and photographing himself wearing the underwear of female residents. In 2009, he started to assault women before stealing their underwear, and then moved up to murder, kidnapping a woman on a highway before killing her and ditching her body in a forest. Police secured a tire print near the victim's home, and an officer called out a match on Williams's car at a checkpoint. After ten hours of questioning, Williams confessed.

Only one death has ever been linked to purposely tainted Halloween candy.

In 1974, Texan Ronald O'Bryan handed out Pixy Stix laced with cyanide to five children, including his eight-year-old son, Timothy. He was in the middle of a custody dispute with his former wife and had intended to harm his son to exact revenge on his estranged spouse. Timothy O'Bryan died; Ronald O'Bryan received the death penalty; the other four kids didn't eat the poisoned candy.

Witnesses calling for a killer to leave couldn't dissuade him from completing a murder.

Kitty Genovese returned to her home in Queens, New York, around 3 A.M. on March 13, 1964. Before she could open her door, a man attacked and repeatedly stabbed her. Genovese called out for help in no uncertain terms, yelling, "He stabbed me, please help me!" Several residents awoke, turned on their lights, and opened their windows, with just one man yelling, "Leave that girl alone!" The attacker ran off, but when things quieted down, he returned and stabbed Genovese again. She called for help again, the attacker ran away, and finally, at 3:50 A.M., police were summoned. Genovese died before she made it to the hospital. Nearly forty people had witnessed the assault, and nobody had intervened. It was an example of "diffusion of responsibility"—everyone had assumed someone else would help. "Genovese syndrome" is a term used today to describe why humans become helpless bystanders in urgent situations.

Fingerprinting was first used to convict criminals after a 1905 robbery.

London shopkeeper Thomas Farrow was killed in a stickup gone awry one morning in March 1905, a crime that also involved two men going into Farrow's attached residence to look for cash and viciously beating Anne Farrow. Police had little evidence beyond a greasy fingerprint on an empty cashbox. Fingerprinting was still in its infancy, a novelty in evidence detecting. With neighbors suggesting that the crime was the work of known thieves, Alfred and Albert Stratton, detectives compared the fingerprint on the cashbox with one they had on file of Albert. The prints matched, and it was entered as evidence in the trial of Alfred Stratton. This was the first time that fingerprints were used as evidence in a criminal trial; Stratton was found guilty of murder.

A convicted murderer sued his prison over a bad meal.

Lawrence Bittaker and an accomplice went on a grisly spree in 1979, kidnapping, assaulting, torturing, and then murdering a total of five teenage girls. Decades later, he'd file a lawsuit against the prison where he was serving a life sentence, citing "cruel and unusual punishment." The punishment was this: He'd been served a soggy sandwich and a broken cookie at the prison cafeteria for lunch one day.

The mistress of a powerful White House advisor was murdered after she went public.

Alfred Bloomingdale, heir to the department store fortune and an advisor to President Reagan, kept up a twelve-year affair with model Vicki Morgan, supplying her with a monthly income of $18,000. When Bloomingdale was hospitalized with throat cancer, wife Betsy Bloomingdale put an end to the dalliance and cut off Morgan financially. Morgan threatened to publish a memoir about her affair, but she was strong-armed by the White House against doing so, and instead filed a $10 million palimony suit, revealing all of Bloomingdale's violent sexual habits. In July 1983, Morgan was found in her apartment beaten to death. Her roommate, Marvin Pancoast, confessed, although he also confessed to crimes that he had nothing to do with, like the Manson family murders. Authorities theorize that someone in Bloomingdale's powerful circle had Morgan killed before she could cause more embarrassment.

One man blew up an airplane full of people just to kill his mother.

Jack Gilbert Graham is classified as a mass murderer. He was sentenced to death for placing a bomb onboard United flight 629 in November 1955, killing forty-four people. He was only after one person, though: his mother, Daisie Graham. He saw her off on her flight, then purchased a life insurance policy on her from an airport vending machine. The time bomb he'd placed in her suitcase exploded when the plane was in the air over Colorado.

Two rich college students murdered a child just to see if they could.

In 1924, the body of fourteen-year-old Bobby Franks was discovered in a culvert in Wolf Lake, Indiana, having been struck with a blunt object and then suffocated to death. A pair of eyeglasses were discovered and were traced to nineteen-year-old Nathan Leopold, a close friend of Franks's cousin, Richard Loeb. Under intense questioning, both Nathan and Richard, who were from wealthy families and studied at the prestigious University of Chicago, confessed. The reason they killed Franks: to prove that they could get away with it and demonstrate that they were innately superior human beings. Not even an impassioned defense could save Leopold and Loeb. Instead of his clients pleading guilty by reason of insanity as expected, their attorney took a risk and entered a guilty plea. He argued that his clients were "emotionally diseased" and hoped the judge would be lenient. It didn't work—they both got life sentences. Loeb was murdered in prison in 1936; Leopold was paroled in 1958.

One of the Menendez brothers depicted his crimes in a screenplay he wrote.

Erik and Lyle Menendez murdered their parents in their Los Angeles home, not far from Hollywood, where Erik dreamed of being a screenwriter. Years before he helped kill his parents, he wrote a screenplay called *Friends* about a boy who murders his wealthy parents to collect on a lucrative life insurance policy. The first five pages detail the exact murder scene that transpired when the Menendez parents died.

The murdering Menendez brothers cameoed on a trading card.

Erik and Lyle Menendez were convicted of murdering their wealthy parents to more quickly inherit their fortune. An odd relic of the case popped up on a basketball trading card, which wasn't widely noticed for nearly thirty years. New York Knicks star Mark Jackson's 1990 NBA Hoops card features an action shot from a game played in Los Angeles. The Menendez brothers are clearly visible sitting courtside. The image was taken during the 1989–90 NBA season—after the August 20, 1989, murders, but before the brothers were arrested in March 1990.

Lyle Menendez has gotten married, divorced, and married again, all while in prison.

Along with his brother, Erik, Lyle Menendez was found guilty of the murder of his parents. His motive: to inherit their money as fast as possible. During his life sentence, he struck up a correspondence with Anna Eriksson, later marrying her. Eriksson filed for and was granted a divorce, however, when she learned that Menendez had been cheating on her—as he'd started up a new pen-pal relationship with another woman. Menendez then married *that* woman, Rebecca Sneed, while still behind bars.

A family that appeared on *Wife Swap* was annihilated by one of its own.

The Stockdale family of Beach City, Ohio, were a staunchly traditional family when they appeared on the reality show *Wife Swap* in 2008, showing off their farm and homestead and raising their four sons with strict rules that included no TV or dating, and mandatory participation in the family clog-dance troupe. In 2017, Stark County police received a silent 911 call from the Stockdale home and heard a gunshot as they arrived. They soon discovered that one of the boys, Jacob Stockdale, had killed his mother and brother James before turning the gun on himself. He survived the suicide attempt, was tried for murder, and attempted to escape from his mental hospital twice while awaiting trial.

A hypnotist persuaded a man to kill, but he still got in trouble for it.

A wealthy Kansas landowner named Anderson Gray was in the midst of a lawsuit in 1894, and associate Thomas Patton was scheduled to testify against him. Gray decided to have Patton murdered before he could do so, and he hired Wichita farmer Thomas McDonald to do the dirty work. Gray reportedly hypnotized McDonald, gave him a rifle, and drove him to Patton's house, where the hypnotized man carried out the murder. Though McDonald was prosecuted and tried for murder, he was acquitted on the grounds that he'd been hypnotized and hadn't acted on his own volition. In the end, Gray was convicted of the murder.

There's a small plot of American land where murder is hard to prosecute.

Inside the vast, multiple-states-spanning Yellowstone National Park is a fifty-mile zone that is also a legal gray area. Because it's part of a national park, it's federal land, so theoretically, any crime committed there would be a federal crime, and the defendant entitled to a trial by jury of local residents. But since nobody lives in that part of Yellowstone, and because it's also state land as well as federal land, no jury could be assembled, so no trial could take place, making any crime, even murder, difficult to prosecute. (Fortunately, no such crimes have ever been committed here.)

Robert Durst set himself up for capture.

The 2015 HBO documentary series *The Jinx: The Life and Deaths of Robert Durst* familiarized the world with the title subject, a New York real estate scion connected to, and accused of committing, three murders in thirty years. In the finale of the show, Durst doesn't realize his microphone is live, and he says, "What the hell did I do? Killed them all, of course." Six years after *The Jinx* aired, Durst was convicted of one of those murders and sentenced to life without parole, a legal development that came about because of his admission of guilt on the TV series he commissioned filmmakers to create.

A man was murdered by his wife's lover, who secretly lived in the attic.

In August 1922, police discovered wealthy textile manager Fred Oesterreich dead in his Los Angeles home from a gunshot wound. His wife of twenty-five years, Dolly, was found in a locked cupboard, unnerved but unharmed. It seemed as if Fred had been killed in a burglary gone wrong, but, strangely, no possessions had been taken. Years later, the truth emerged: There was no burglary. Dolly had been carrying on an affair for nine years with a repairman named Otto Sanhuber, who'd been hired by Fred. He secretly lived in the Oesterreich's attic for years until he emerged and shot Fred three times in the chest when he heard the couple fighting. The lovers staged the scene to look like a robbery.

There's a difference between mass murderers, serial killers, and spree killers.

All three types of high-volume murderers kill a lot of people, but the FBI and other crime-fighting bodies define them by their approach. Mass murderers kill a bunch of people all at once, and only once—like in a public shooting. Serial killers kill one person at a time, and each murder is followed by a cooling-off period. Spree killers commit multiple murders in multiple locations over a brief period of time.

A damning true crime book was intended to serve as an exoneration.

In February 1970, U.S. Army captain and doctor Jeffrey R. MacDonald killed his wife and children in their home on a base in Fort Bragg, North Carolina. It took years for investigators to build a solid case against him, but eventually they did. He was convicted of the crimes in 1979 and sentenced to life in prison. MacDonald asserted his innocence throughout, despite overwhelming evidence that he committed the murders. He even hired a journalist to write a book to exonerate him to try and turn the tide of the public opinion. Instead, the writer of the book *Fatal Vision*, Joe McGinniss, became positive that MacDonald was guilty, and the book became a true crime bestseller, for which MacDonald sued McGinniss.

Criminal profiling dates to the nineteenth century.

The first to study criminology and serial murder was Dr. Richard von Krafft-Ebing, who conducted research on sexual offenders so as to profile them and understand them. He wrote his findings in the 1886 textbook *Psychopathia Sexualis*, which for decades was the definitive psychological text on sexual deviancy. He persuaded law enforcement officials to consider the state of mind of killers before delivering sentencing. (Von Krafft-Ebing's book also coined the words *sadist*, *masochist*, and *necrophilia*.)

Autopsies have been successfully performed for centuries.

The first autopsies on record were informally performed by embalmers in ancient Egypt, who, during the mummification process, removed and examined organs to look for defect or signs of foul play. The first recorded autopsy was that of Julius Caesar, which revealed that he'd been stabbed twenty-three times, with the fatal wound being the one that pierced his heart. Forensics wouldn't be used to solve crime until the process was popularized in the late nineteenth century by Sir Arthur Conan Doyle's Sherlock Holmes stories.

A Kansas City killer murdered anyone if he suspected them of prostitution.

Terry Blair is the rare girlfriend killer *and* serial killer, although both are linked by one thing: a vicious and violent hatred of prostitutes. He suspected Angela Monroe (his girlfriend) of that profession (for no good reason), and murdered her in cold blood. He served his twenty-one years in prison, then went on a tear while on parole, killing two prostitutes in Kansas City. After he killed the women, he called 911 to report it, but the police had already found the corpses.

A Dallas killer was obsessed with eyeballs.

There was one bizarre link between the murders of three Dallas prostitutes in 1991: They were missing an eyeball. Eventually, a hair found on a victim was traced to Charles Albright, who was convicted and given a life sentence for just one of the murders. In his cell, his favorite pastime was drawing pictures of eyeballs to hang on the walls.

The D.C. Beltway Sniper was actually two people.

In 2002, the D.C. Beltway Sniper killed seventeen people and hurt ten others by shooting them with a long-distance rifle. Creepy clues were left at the scenes of some murders, including the "Death" tarot card, a note that said, "Call me God," and a three-page note demanding $10 million. In a traced phone call, the sniper mentioned an unsolved murder in Montgomery, Alabama. They were able to link that murder to two people: John Allen Muhammad *and* Lee Boyd Malvo. Muhammad got the death penalty, Malvo life in prison.

Not all states guarantee a last meal.

The centuries-old tradition of giving a prisoner a final meal before he or she is executed is not followed in every state. Men and women awaiting execution in Texas get the regular cafeteria food like everyone else. In Florida, prisoners get a $40 budget for their last meal, but that's not the case in Oklahoma, where the budget caps out at $25.

Child killer Westley Allan Dodd was caught when he got too brazen.

Westley Allan Dodd abducted, assaulted, tortured, murdered, and abandoned the bodies of three boys in Vancouver, Washington, in 1989. He was arrested when he was thwarted trying to abduct his fourth victim. He walked into a movie theater and brazenly attempted to pick up a boy and leave with him. He would eventually be hanged, the first hanging in thirty years in the U.S.

The electric chair was supposed to be a kinder form of execution.

William Kemmler goes down in history for a shocking reason: He was the first person to receive capital punishment by electric chair, a method that was introduced as a more humane and efficient way to execute someone (when compared to a firing squad or hanging). Kemmler murdered his mistress during a fight in New York in 1890, two years after the chair was introduced (bad timing for him).

An Illinois man was exonerated and pardoned after he died.

Grover Thompson was sentenced to forty years in prison for the attempted murder of Ida White in Mount Vernon, Illinois, in 1981. His health rapidly declined while in prison. By 1993, he needed a wheelchair to get around. He died in 1996. In 2007, more than a decade after Thompson died in prison, serial killer Timothy Krajcir confessed to stabbing White. Thompson was innocent and received a posthumous pardon, an Illinois first.

A violent criminal got busted after an accidental phone call.

In 2013, Scott Simon got into a fight in a parking lot with his girlfriend in tow. His girlfriend had accidentally "butt-dialed" 911 with her phone in her pocket. When he told his friends to shoot the other guy, the police were on the line listening.

Quincy Green thwarted his ankle-monitor restrictions because he had a prosthetic leg.

It was 2016 when, already on house arrest and being monitored by an electronic ankle bracelet, Quincy Green left his home, committed a murder, and was convicted of doing so. How did he do it? He had a prosthetic leg. Parole department officials had no idea that they'd placed the monitoring device on a false, removable leg, and Green took it off and replaced it with a free and easy backup when he needed to leave home.

A hotel's water problems hinted at a grisly discovery to come.

Canadian tourist Elisa Lam took a solo trip in 2013 to Los Angeles, where she stayed at the Cecil Hotel, a shabby establishment downtown. When she didn't check out and didn't call home, the LAPD got involved. Two weeks went by, and no trace of her was found. After hotel guests complained about the black and foul-tasting water, and the sudden drop in water pressure, staff investigated and found, in the rooftop water tank, the body of Lam. It was never discovered how she could have gotten access to the roof, climbed into the tank, or shut the heavy lid. But elevator security footage shows her waving her arms and acting afraid, talking to someone not captured on camera.

The O.J. Simpson police chase could have ended earlier and with more violence.

The reason that O. J. Simpson's car chase with Los Angeles police in 1994 was so slow was that his friend, Al Cowlings, was driving Simpson's car. Simpson sat in the passenger seat with a gun to his own head threatening suicide. Cowlings and police figured if they sped up, or stopped, Simpson would pull the trigger.

Dog bones prevented dogs from finding the remains of Dorothy Scott.

In May 1980, Dorothy Scott disappeared from the parking lot of an Anaheim, California, hospital, where her car was stolen by her abductor. Her badly decomposed body wasn't found for four years, when it was discovered to be charred from a wildfire and covered with the bones of a dead dog to throw off police dogs tracking Scott's scent. Dental records identified the body, but the remains were in such a poor state that no actual cause of death could be determined.

Dorothy Scott's murderer knew how to befuddle call-tracing technology.

The man believed to be the perpetrator of the murder of Dorothy Scott taunted the public and law enforcement officials. An anonymous person called the *Orange County Register* and told an editor that he killed Dorothy Scott, his lover, because he had caught her cheating and she had denied the affair. He knew many personal details about Scott's life and her activities the night she disappeared. The same man also delivered taunting phone calls to Scott's mother, taking credit for the murder, but he never stayed on the line long enough for the calls to be traced.

An escaped murderer merely escaped inside the crime scene.

After murdering a pregnant preschool teacher and her two children in Massachusetts in 1987, Daniel LaPlante absconded, disappearing from police protection. Weeks later, he materialized in the home—specifically in the closet—of a woman he once dated wearing makeup and her mother's clothes and wielding a knife. LaPlante tied up the woman, her parents, and her sister, who escaped and freed everyone else. Another two weeks went by and LaPlante again disappeared. The family, who had temporarily relocated, went back to the house where LaPlante had tormented them and saw LaPlante inside. Police were summoned, and they eventually determined that he'd been living in the walls of the house since immediately after the murders.

Charles Manson got other people to do his murdering for him.

The Tate-LaBianca murders, in which the Manson Family death cult killed Sharon Tate and four others on August 8, 1969, and Leno and Rosemary LaBianca the next day, were not actually committed by Charles Manson himself. He gave the orders to his brainwashed followers. Tex Watson, Leslie Van Houten, Patricia Krenwinkel, and Susan Atkins committed the brutal slayings while Manson watched.

A baseball accident led to the hasty murder of a Florida child.

The story of a missing eight-year-old from Jacksonville, Florida, named Maddie Clifton made national news in 1998, with a regional search that went on for a week after her disappearance. She hadn't gone far, as it turned out. Fourteen-year-old neighbor Joshua Phillips had been playing baseball with Clifton when he accidentally hit her with a ball, causing her to bleed around the eye, and cry and wail uncontrollably. Phillips, panicked that Clifton was seriously hurt and fearing retribution from his abusive father, took Clifton into his bedroom, stabbed her eleven times, and beat her with a baseball bat. Then he hid the body under his bed, where it was discovered by his mother when he was at school.

A mass-shooting perpetrator was held responsible for a death thirty years after the fact.

Charles Whitman, the man who climbed into the clock tower at the University of Texas in Austin and started shooting people below at random, is often cited as the first modern-day public mass shooter. He killed fourteen people that day in 1966 before a police sniper took him out. And yet, thirty-five years later, Whitman was found liable for a fifteenth fatality. David Gunby survived the shooting after taking a bullet to the kidney that would leave him on dialysis for the rest of his life. His life ended prematurely in 2001 because of his condition. Authorities cited Whitman as the perpetrator of his death.

A single tragic murder led to the inception of Megan's Law.

In 1994, seven-year-old Megan Kanka was sexually assaulted and then murdered by her neighbor, Jesse Timmendequas. Unbeknownst to Kanka's family, Timmendequas was a parolee who had already served time for sex crimes committed against minors. Kanka's parents said they never would have allowed their daughter to play outside or walk around the neighborhood had they known, and Megan's death led to the passage of Megan's Law, which requires sex offenders on parole to register with police and neighbors when they move into a new area.

Jake Bird set a record for most last meals.

Originally convicted of a 1947 murder in Washington state, Jake Bird received three last-minute stays of execution, with the governor's call saving him from the electric chair three times after he'd had his last meal and was being prepped for the gallows. Finally, after last meal number four, Bird was hanged for being identified as the man who killed a woman named Bertha Kludt with an ax.

Some death row inmates have cracked jokes with their last words.

Convicted, condemned murderers are usually given the opportunity to provide a final statement or "last words" to family, witnesses, and the media moments before their execution. Sometimes they use the chance to crack wise. When George Appel was placed in the electric chair in 1928 for killing a police officer, his last words were, "Well, gentlemen, you are about to see a baked Appel." Similarly, when two-time murderer James French was set to be executed via electrocution in 1966, he quipped, "How's this for a headline? 'French Fries.' "

James French pleaded for his own execution.

While hitchhiking through Oklahoma in 1958, James French took a ride from and then killed motorist Frank Boone. French actually asked for the death penalty, but the jury gave him a life sentence. Undeterred, he unsuccessfully petitioned Oklahoma's governor's office for his sentence to be upgraded to a death sentence. In 1961, French was paired with a new cellmate, Eddie Lee Shelton. They didn't get along. French attacked and killed Shelton, strangling him with a towel wrapped around his neck. It was then that French got his wish. The state went ahead and changed that life sentence to a death sentence.

A murderer who fled tried to evade capture with suicide but failed.

In 1981, Ricky Ray Rector killed a man in an Arkansas restaurant, then fled. After three days in hiding and on the lam, he negotiated his surrender with authorities in Conway, Arkansas, but in a last-minute turn of events, he decided to shoot the negotiating police officer, killing him. Rector then tried to commit suicide via gunshot to the head, but he lived, albeit suffering severe intellectual limitations thereafter, the effects likened to those of a lobotomy.

Ricky Ray Rector wanted to save part of his last meal for after the execution.

Ricky Ray Rector was sentenced to death by lethal injection in 1992, despite the protests of anti–death penalty advocates who held that executing the convict was inhumane and cruel, owing to his mental deficiencies. Rector's last meal request and behavior hinted at his inability to grasp the seriousness of the situation. He dined on steak, chicken, and Kool-Aid, and asked for his dessert, a slice of pecan pie, to be set aside "for later," meaning after his lethal injection.

A gang-shooting perpetrator commemorated the event on his body.

LAPD homicide investigators had a difficult time finding a suspect in the 2004 murder of a known gang member outside of a Los Angeles liquor store. Years later, they got a lead when Anthony Garcia, a member of the victim's rival gang, was picked up on another charge. Police took photos of his elaborate chest tattoo, which depicted the liquor store shooting in explicit detail, but no one connected it to the specific murder right away. Two years later, investigators were looking through gang tattoo photo logs and made the connection. In 2011, Garcia was convicted of first-degree murder and sentenced to sixty-five years in prison.

A crowdsourced crime-solving website ensnared a murderer.

Tricia Griffith helped start Websleuth in 2004, and by 2009, the online crime discussion site had plumbed the mysterious death of Abraham Shakespeare, a day laborer turned $32 million lottery winner. The murder investigation focused heavily on his financial advisor, Dee Dee Moore. Websleuth users so vehemently called out Moore that she registered for the site under a fake name and launched an online defense of herself. Eventually, Griffith discovered that an email Moore sent her, telling her to get Websleuth to back off, had the same IP address as the Moore "defender," meaning both messages came from the same computer. That launched an official police investigation into Moore's role in Shakespeare's murder. She was, in the end, convicted of the crime.

A secret witness led to the conviction of mass murderer Richard Speck.

On July 14, 1966, Richard Speck invaded a townhouse in Chicago where nine young women in nursing school all resided. Speck held them at knifepoint, then took each woman into a room and methodically killed them all via strangulation or stabbing. His last victim was raped and strangled. Speck fled and was captured a few days later after being treated for a suicide attempt at a Chicago hospital, where a doctor recognized him from a police sketch. Speck didn't know that he hadn't killed everyone in the home: Corazon Amurao hid under a bed during Speck's murder spree, and her testimony both identified and helped convict him.

A renowned forensic artist got into that line of work because of a personal assault.

Lois Gibson is a Guinness World Records holder for being the most successful forensic artist in history, as measured by the number of crimes she's helped police solve. Working with the Houston Police Department, she's drawn up composite sketches and other crime-solving visual aids that have led to arrests and closure in more than 1,000 cases. Gibson was personally motivated by a nearly fatal choking and sexual assault, and after witnessing her attacker get arrested, she wanted to help bring criminals to justice.

A juror was murdered during Richard Ramirez's murder trial.

During an early hearing in the 1989 murder trial of Richard Ramirez, "the Night Stalker," a juror named Phyllis Singletary failed to report for duty one morning, and later that day was found in her apartment dead of a gunshot wound. Authorities and the rest of the jury were worried that Ramirez had somehow committed an act of jury intimidation by way of murder, but it was just a gruesome and sad coincidence. Singletary had been shot by her boyfriend, who killed himself two days after the murder.

A man killed his entire family during an Easter celebration.

Awaking from a nap on Easter 1975 after a night of drinking, James Urban Ruppert loaded the four guns he'd brought with him to his mother's house in Hamilton, Ohio, and in less than five minutes, he killed eleven members of his family: his mother, brother, sister-in-law, and eight nieces and nephews. And then he sat in the house for three hours before calling police, saying, "There's been a shooting."

One of the Oklahoma City bombers was caught because of a minor driving infraction.

Timothy McVeigh led the party that planted a truck of explosives at the Murrah Federal Building in Oklahoma City in 1995, the worst domestic terrorist act in U.S. history to that point with a death toll of 168 (including 19 children) and 800 injuries. McVeigh did little to cover his tracks in his politically motivated crime. He rented the truck, which was easily traceable to him, and was captured by a state trooper when he was driving a car with no registration tag.

A tight end played in the NFL after committing two murders.

Aaron Hernandez played tight end for the NFL's New England Patriots between 2010 and 2013. His final professional football game was a season-ending playoff loss in January 2013. The following year, he was indicted for murder. He was convicted in the shooting death of semipro football player Odin Lloyd in April 2015. Hernandez was also indicted in connection with a drive-by shooting in 2012 that left two men dead, but was later acquitted of the crime. He committed suicide in his jail cell on April 19, 2017. An autopsy revealed that Hernandez had the most severe form of CTE (a degenerative brain disease known to affect judgment) that researchers had ever seen in a twenty-seven-year-old.

Joseph Borowiak went out for pizza while covered in his victims' blood.

Joseph Borowiak unabashedly left a host of evidence in his wake after shooting and killing his aunt and uncle (who had raised him) in their Michigan home in 2017. Immediately after the death, he described it on social media, publicly posted his list of who he planned to kill next, and then went and got a pizza with blood all over his shirt and glasses. Borowiak also thought he was God and kept an altar in his basement.

The lethal injection was introduced in the early 1980s.

Oklahoma's state medical examiner, Jay Chapman, devised a new form of capital punishment, or an execution method known at first as "Chapman's protocol." In the interest of finding a less painful and more efficient way to end the lives of death row inmates, Chapman proposed having an intravenous saline drip put into the prisoner's arm. A "lethal injection" of barbiturates and a paralytic could be delivered through the drip. The Oklahoma state government adopted the method into law in 1977. Texas soon followed suit, and in 1982, convicted murderer Charles Brooks Jr. was the first prisoner to be executed with lethal injection.

The guillotine was used well into the 1970s.

Hamida Djandoubi emigrated from his native Tunisia to Marseilles, France, at age nineteen in 1968 to work in agriculture. In 1974, he turned to violent crime, kidnapping, torturing, and murdering Elisabeth Bousquet. A French judge gave Djandoubi the death penalty in February 1977, and that September, he was executed by guillotine. He has the twisted honor of being the last person to be killed via guillotine and was the last person in the world beheaded by an official state order.

Two murderers tried to avoid ratting each other out, and both paid the price.

In December 1976, Charles Brooks Jr. asked to test-drive a car at a Fort Worth, Texas, used-car lot. Mechanic David Gregory went along, and Brooks drove Gregory to pick up Brooks's friend, Woody Loudres. At some point, Loudres helped him throw Gregory into the trunk. Then they went to a motel, bound and gagged the mechanic, and shot him fatally in the head. Neither Loudres nor Brooks would say who actually pulled the trigger, so a Texas court gave them both the death penalty. Brooks was executed by lethal injection for his crime, and would admit on tape just before his death to pulling the trigger. Loudres's conviction would eventually be overturned in the appeals process. He'd be paroled after serving only eleven years.

A Dutch murderer willingly gave an incriminating DNA sample to the government.

Police in the Holland region of the Netherlands were stymied by a 1999 murder case that quickly went cold and was still unsolved by 2012. That's when police publicly asked all men who lived within a five-mile radius of where the crime had occurred to willingly submit a saliva DNA sample. More than 6,600 Dutch men did their civic duty, including the man whose DNA lined up with that left behind by the murderer.

A Texas man had his family killed right after his own graduation party.

After returning home from celebrating the 2003 college graduation of their son Bart with a big dinner, three people in the Whitaker family—Bart's brother, mother, and father—were shot by a stranger in a home invasion and robbery turned violent. Only Bart and his father survived. An investigation found that Bart Whitaker had hired the gunman to off his family members, and Bart received the death sentence. Whitaker was never executed, because his own father aggressively advocated for a commutation to life in prison, granted moments before Whitaker's scheduled death in Texas in 2007.

Los Angeles police followed around a suspect until he spat on the ground.

Police in the Los Angeles area found common suspect DNA at two crime scenes in 2011: the scene of the assault and murder of Michelle Lozano, and the site where Bree'Anna Guzman was murdered. Authorities were almost entirely sure that a man named Geovanni Borjas had committed the crimes, but to confirm their suspicions, they'd need a DNA sample from him. So they secretly followed him around until they saw him spit on the ground. They collected the spit, tested it, found that it matched, and arrested him.

An Oakland band drummed up publicity by linking themselves to a murder.

Experimental musical collective Negativland had an unexpected hit album in 1987 with *Escape from Noise*, but plans to tour were canceled, according to a press release issued by the band. The press release claimed that a federal agent had barred them from playing live because their song "Christianity Is Stupid" had driven sixteen-year-old David Brom to kill his parents, brother, and sister with an ax. Negativland denied inspiring Brom—because they hadn't. They'd fabricated the news about the ban, and the connection to Brom, to drum up publicity.

A man's Tinder activity led to his capture by authorities.

There's some measure of safety in using smartphone dating apps to connect with strangers who could very well be criminals. Every "match" leaves a digital record of the connection between parties. In 2018, Danueal Drayton strangled Samantha Stewart at her home in New York, having matched with her on Tinder. Then he moved to Los Angeles, and two weeks later, assaulted, held captive, and tried to murder a second woman. After he was arrested, it was relatively easy for investigators to get into Drayton's Tinder account and connect him to the two victims.

A questionable prison errand allows a murderer to avoid serving time.

Leonard T. Fristoe killed two people and was sentenced to life behind bars in a Nevada prison in 1920. Three years into his term, he escaped while driving the prison warden to an area brothel. Fristoe avoided capture for more than four decades, turning himself in to authorities in 1966, at age seventy-seven, telling a judge he wanted to return to prison to "get it over with." After five months back in prison, he was pardoned by the governor and released.

Welsh killer George Johnson killed twice for pocket money.

Many criminals kill for money, but few killed for as little as Welshman George Johnson. In 1986, Johnson and an accomplice followed a man home one night and stabbed him with a knife and scissors until he was dead, just so they could rob him of the £3 in his pocket. In 2003, Johnson was released, and soon became addicted to heroin. To get the money for his next fix, he beat an eighty-nine-year-old woman to death to steal her two pieces of jewelry and the £25 on her person.

The likely killer of Natalee Holloway was jailed for a different crime.

The son of a wealthy Dutch-Aruban lawyer, Joran van der Sloot was linked to the disappearance and presumed murder of American student Natalee Holloway, who vanished during a senior class trip to Aruba in 2005. While arrested but never charged, Van der Sloot reportedly privately took credit for Holloway's demise, alternately confessing that he sold her into a sexual slavery ring, or threw her body into the ocean. He was ultimately charged with extortion when he attempted to lure money from the Holloway family in exchange for information about where he had put her body. Van der Sloot would wind up in prison in the end, but not for killing Holloway. In 2010, he was convicted of murder in Peru for the death of Stephany Ramirez.

A privileged child of wealth killed his father when he threatened to pull his financial support.

Wealthy, powerful New York hedge fund manager Thomas Gilbert Sr. was found dead in his Manhattan apartment in 2015, a gunshot wound to his head. His wife, Shelley, had just left the residence to go buy a sandwich at the behest of her son, Thomas Gilbert Jr., who took the opportunity to kill his father. The reason: Gilbert Sr. threatened to cut off Gilbert Jr. from the hefty allowance that he'd been living off for years.

It took three decades to convict a Kennedy relative of murder.

Michael Skakel is a member of the prominent and legendary Kennedy political family. He's the nephew of Ethel Kennedy, wife of Robert F. Kennedy. In the mid-1970s, fifteen-year-old Skakel lived in the same Greenwich, Connecticut, neighborhood as fifteen-year-old Martha Moxley, who was discovered in her backyard bludgeoned to death with a golf club in 1975. The last time she was seen alive, she was at the Skakel home, and police initially thought Skakel's brother was the most likely culprit. The case went cold, and it wasn't solved until 2002, when Michael Skakel was found guilty of murder and sentenced to twenty-seven years in prison.

CHAPTER 2

SERIAL KILLERS

Fascinating facts about the most
demented repeat offenders out there,
the ones for whom killing
(and torturing) is a compulsion.

A church computer brought down the BTK Killer.

Ten people in Wichita and Park City, Kansas, died at the hands of the BTK Killer, with BTK short for the killer's process of "bind, torture, kill." In 2004, the anonymous murderer sent a letter to police, asking if floppy disks were traceable; the police publicly stated they weren't, prompting the murderer to send a disk to a Wichita TV station. The police lied. They easily traced the disk to Christ Lutheran Church, where a man named Dennis Rader served as president of the church council. A quick search uncovered more evidence that Rader was the BTK Killer.

The BTK Killer helped protect citizens from the BTK Killer.

When the anonymous BTK serial murderer was "binding, torturing, and killing" victims around Wichita and Park City, Kansas, in the 1970s, it unleashed such fear and precaution that many locals installed home security systems. A man named Dennis Rader worked for a company that installed many of those alarms. The residents could not have imagined that the BTK Killer, the murderer himself, would be their installer.

A subliminal messaging campaign wasn't effective in nailing the BTK Killer.

After the BTK Killer's first wave of brutal murders in the 1970s, Wichita TV station KAKE worked with police to place a subliminal message in a news broadcast about the criminal to urge him to turn himself in. Appearing on screen for a few frames were the words "Now call the chief" and the image of upside-down eyeglasses, like those found near the murdered body of Nancy Fox. It didn't work: Dennis Rader wasn't identified as the BTK Killer until 2005.

A slice of pizza in the trash led to the arrest of a Los Angeles serial killer.

The Grim Sleeper killed ten women in Los Angeles between 1984 and 1988, and from 2002 to 2007. Detectives had little evidence of the murderer, but they did find some DNA when they discovered a new victim in a garbage bag in 2007. That genetic material was matched to some of the 1980s' cold cases, and then to a young man picked up on an illegal weapons charge. The LAPD obtained saliva from a piece of pizza discarded by that individual's father and found that it contained DNA matching that of the Grim Sleeper. Lonnie David Franklin was arrested and received the death penalty.

Jeffrey Dahmer was caught because his would-be eighteenth victim fought him off.

One night in July 1991, Jeffrey Dahmer approached Tracy Edwards in a Milwaukee bar and asked if he'd like to model nude for him. Back at his apartment, Dahmer threatened Edwards with a knife, and handcuffed him. After five hours, he managed to escape, punching Dahmer in the face and running out of the apartment and down the street, where he was picked up by two patrol policemen. They returned to the scene of the crime and uncovered the grisly evidence of seventeen murders, including severed heads in the freezer.

Police interrupted one of Jeffrey Dahmer's murders.

Years before his final arrest in 1991, police were called to the home of Jeffrey Dahmer, after a neighbor called to report the nude and bleeding Konerak Sinthasomphone in the vicinity. The neighbor pleaded with police, saying this was a violent criminal, but they threatened to arrest him for interference and being a nuisance. They believed Dahmer, that the fourteen-year-old was his lover and was upset after a drunken argument. He immediately was returned to Dahmer, who killed him.

Jeffrey Dahmer was murdered in prison.

Christopher Scarver was in the same Wisconsin prison as Jeffrey Dahmer. The cannibalistic serial killer was known for being unrepentant, teasing other inmates, and unnerving those around him when he'd form little arms and legs from his prison food. But when Scarver, also a convicted murderer, got face-to-face with Dahmer for the first time in 1994, Dahmer didn't stand a chance. They were assigned to clean a bathroom together. When Dahmer teased Scarver, Scarver followed him into a locker room, crushed his head with a metal bar, and killed him. Scarver believes that the guards left him alone with Dahmer on purpose.

Jeffrey Dahmer was restrained after he was dead.

While Jeffrey Dahmer had been bludgeoned to death and didn't have a pulse when he left prison, he was taken to a forensic pathologist for an autopsy. Even though he was dead, he was still shackled. The pathologist, Dr. Robert Huntington, said in an interview, "Such was the fear of this man that chains were on the feet, even post mortem."

Dahmer could have been stopped.

Jeffrey Dahmer was once pulled over by police when he was drifting across a center line, suspected of drunk driving. He'd already killed one person, and the victim's remains were in the car. The police noticed the smell and said something, but Dahmer said the smell was from bags of trash he'd forgotten to take to the dump. After Dahmer's capture, the lead investigator found this detail in the old drunk driving report. Further investigation determined that Dahmer's victim had been in the car, and the patrol officer let a mass murderer go.

Dahmer's murderous impulses may have been inherited.

After he'd been imprisoned for multiple murders, Jeffrey Dahmer learned that he may have inherited the predilection to kill from his father. Lionel Dahmer wrote *A Father's Story* and published it in 1994. In it, he admits to adolescent fantasies of murder and a fascination with bombs and fire, but says he never acted on any of them.

A serial killer competed on *The Dating Game*.

In addition to numerous murders and assaults in which he was implicated, Rodney James Alcala was convicted of murdering five people in California between 1977 and 1979 and was sentenced to death. Right in the middle of his terrifying rape and murder spree (in which he extensively photographed his victims), Alcala appeared as a contestant on *The Dating Game*. He was identified on the game show as a "successful photographer" who liked to skydive and ride his motorcycle. The episode's bachelorette selected the murderer to be her date, but never went through with it because she found Alcala "creepy."

An Uber driver in Michigan went on a killing spree.

Jason Dalton worked as an Uber driver in Kalamazoo, Michigan. One day in February 2016, the company and the local 911 dispatch fielded numerous complaint calls about Dalton, citing dangerous and erratic driving. Uber was urged to change its background check and emergency reporting policies after Dalton's behavior later that day when he went on a shooting spree that left six people dead and two others critically injured.

Rodney Alcala defended himself in court.

Rodney Alcala declined his right to an attorney, even a state-appointed one, when on trial for his various murders in California. He acted as his own lawyer instead, and actually interrogated himself on the witness stand, addressing "Mr. Alcala" in a booming voice, and then answering himself in his normal voice. (He was convicted anyway.)

A lack of license plates on his car nailed serial killer Joel Rifkin.

Many serial killers will fulfill their pathological need to kill—and avoid capture—by targeting prostitutes, drug addicts, and others who fall through the cracks of society and can go missing without sounding as many alarms. Joel Rifkin did just that, murdering as many as seventeen drug-addicted sex workers in New York City and Long Island between 1989 and 1993. He was captured not because of evidence of his violent crimes, but because he neglected to put license plates on his car. Stopped by police for driving without plates, Rifkin panicked and engaged authorities in a high-speed pursuit that ended when he crashed into a pole outside a courthouse where he'd later stand trial and receive a 203-year prison sentence.

Joel Rifkin wanted to reform prostitutes.

Shortly after he was apprehended for murdering somewhere between nine and seventeen women in New York from 1989 to 1993, Joel Rifkin was sentenced to 203 years in prison. Six years in, in 1999, he submitted to prison officials a ten-page proposal to open a rehabilitative shelter for prostitutes, a group that he had once targeted as victims. His facility would offer drug treatment, job training, and counseling. "It's a way of paying back a debt, I guess," Rifkin said at the time. He also suggested a "scared straight" program where prostitutes would see dead sex workers at a morgue. The plan was not adopted.

His own plumbing complaints got the Muswell Hill Murderer captured.

Between 1978 and 1983, serial murderer Denis Nilsen killed twelve men in a London neighborhood. He became known as the Muswell Hill Murderer. He'd strangle his victims, then keep their bodies in his apartment, eventually dissecting them and burning most of their remains. Authorities apprehended him after Nilsen and others in his building called a plumber complaining of clogged drains. The plumbers traced the blockages to the top-floor apartment, where Nilsen lived, and found that the blockages consisted of flesh and human bone pieces. Nilsen confessed to police, who discovered bags of human remains in his home, and he was arrested and sentenced to life in prison.

After an NFL career didn't work out, a football player became a serial killer.

Randall Woodfield was both a football star and a criminal as a teenager. The wide receiver for Newport High School in Oregon in the late 1960s also got arrested on a charge of indecent exposure. He went on to play for Portland State University and was drafted by the Green Bay Packers, but he was cut during training camp after being repeatedly arrested for indecent exposure. In 1975 he returned to Oregon, where he was linked to multiple robberies and knifepoint sexual assaults. From 1980 to 1981, he killed as many as forty-four people in the Pacific Northwest.

Genealogy websites brought down the Golden State Killer.

Between 1974 and 1986, a man known alternately as the Visalia Ransacker, the East Area Rapist, the Original Night Stalker, and the Golden State Killer terrorized different areas of Northern California. Over three different crime sprees, he committed 120 burglaries, fifty-one sexual assaults, and at least thirteen murders. Joseph DeAngelo was identified and arrested in 2018, at which point he delivered a full confession. He was caught by authorities using DNA evidence. His genetic material taken from crime scenes matched with that of members of the DeAngelo family on genealogy research websites, and investigators narrowed it down to him.

The Golden State Killer waited for his victims in their bedrooms.

The Golden State Killer, who killed at least thirteen people from 1974 to 1986, wasn't identified until the 2010s as Joseph DeAngelo. A home invader who assaulted women and sometimes killed them, he wouldn't attack people while they slept, but preferred to wait for them to wake up. He'd break into their home, stand at the entrance to their bedroom, and tap his knife against the wall until they woke up.

Serial killer John Wayne Gacy also worked as a party clown.

On July 30, 1999, the *Kansas City Star* made note of how it was National Clown Week with a short article about the heavily made-up children's entertainers. A file photo ran with the piece, and it must have been hastily chosen, or carelessly approved, because it was a photo of long-ago convicted and since-executed Chicago-area serial killer John Wayne Gacy. He worked as a birthday party entertainer named Pogo the Clown between committing more than thirty murders.

Gacy was a prominent and productive man of stature.

John Wayne Gacy is commonly associated with his Pogo the Clown character, but he never killed or lured victims while in his clown makeup and costume. He performed as a birthday party entertainer on weekends, when he wasn't managing a Kentucky Fried Chicken or serving on several Chicagoland business and men's organizations.

A community came together to capture the Night Stalker.

A serial killer known as the Night Stalker haunted nighttime Los Angeles from 1984 to 1985, staging home invasions, sexually assaulting inhabitants, murdering them, and leaving satanic symbols behind. He killed thirteen people and evaded capture, even after the LAPD figured out his identity and plastered the mugshot of Richard Ramirez all over the city. While that unfolded, Ramirez was back home in Arizona, and he didn't know police were closing in. He came into L.A. via a Greyhound bus, walked into a convenience store, and was spotted by an older woman of Latino descent who saw his picture on a newspaper just minutes earlier and shouted *"El maton!"* ("The Killer!"). Ramirez ran away, but after multiple people tried to stop him, he was taken down by an angry mob.

It took years to disentangle the remains of John Wayne Gacy's victims.

John Wayne Gacy killed thirty-three men and boys, and he stuffed the remains of twenty-nine of them into the crawl space beneath his modest, three-bedroom home in the suburbs of Chicago. After he was captured in 1978 and authorities started searching Gacy's property for evidence and the dead bodies, they weren't sure how many deceased individuals were inside of the house. There were so many that the bodies had melted together, and it took forensic specialists more than two years to completely separate and differentiate the twenty-nine skeletons.

John Wayne Gacy lent assistance to a major Hollywood filmmaker.

Punk rock singer GG Allin, of GG Allin and the Murder Junkies, was prone to violent acts and self-harm while performing. Obsessed with death and darkness, he befriended imprisoned serial killer John Wayne Gacy in the 1980s. They were so close that when Todd Phillips, writer and director of such films as *Old School*, *The Hangover*, and *Joker*, was getting his career going in 1993 with the Allin documentary *Hated*, he wrote to Gacy, a jailhouse painter, to see if he would paint a movie poster. Instead, Phillips raised $10,000 by selling some of Gacy's paintings, which covered most of the cost of making *Hated*.

The Night Stalker was a popular prison pen pal.

Awaiting his execution while serving on death row in California's San Quentin prison, Richard Ramirez, "the Night Stalker," regularly received hundreds of letters, almost all of them from women. His most active pen pal (seventy-five letters in all) was a former editor named Doreen Lioy. In 1988, Ramirez proposed, and they married in 1996 at San Quentin. They remained together until Ramirez died in 2013—not of a state-delivered method of execution, but of lymphoma.

Electrical discharge interpreted as God's ire stopped Richard Ramirez from killing a woman.

Richard Ramirez invaded the home of teenager Whitney Bennet in July 1986, savagely beating her with a tire iron. Then he tried to finish her off by strangling her with a telephone cord. When he pulled on the cord, electrical sparks began to shoot out, and it freaked out Ramirez, who took it as a sign from God that Bennet wasn't meant to die. Bennett survived.

Richard Ramirez was nicknamed "the Night Stalker" by the editorial staff of the *Los Angeles Herald Examiner*.

The name had nothing to do with *The Night Stalker*, a cult favorite 1970s TV show about a reporter investigating supernatural killings, nor was there any evidence that Ramirez stalked his victims. The Night Stalker was chosen over other options, like "the Screen-Door Intruder" and "the Walk-In Killer," which more closely described Ramirez's behavior.

How the Son of Sam got his name.

David Berkowitz would eventually be sentenced to life in prison for his six New York City murders from 1976 to 1977. Before he was identified, newspapers called him "the .44 Caliber Killer," after his murder weapon of choice. In 1977, at the scene of a double murder, and in a subsequent letter to the *New York Daily News*, the killer identified himself as Son of Sam—Sam being a demonic spirit that made him murder and had taken up residence in his neighbor's dog. After finding religion in prison in 1987, Berkowitz announced that he preferred to be called Son of Hope.

The Son of Sam was arrested after he illegally parked.

David Berkowitz, a.k.a. the Son of Sam, killed a lot of people in New York City in the late 1970s. He would eventually be found guilty for six of them. In 1977, police responded to a call of gunfire where a witness said she saw a man with a gun running to a cream-colored Ford Galaxie. What set the car apart: It had a parking ticket on the windshield. Detectives simply cross-referenced the car with the records of ones that had been issued parking tickets on the night in question and found it belonged to Berkowitz. With that information, they went to his home and arrested him.

The Oakland County Child Killer gave a victim a notable last meal.

Four children—two boys and two girls—disappeared from Oakland County, Michigan, in 1976 and 1977. During a press conference, the mother of one of the boys pleaded for her child's safe return. She made an offhand comment about wanting to feed him his favorite meal, Kentucky Fried Chicken, when he came home. A few days later, all of the victims' bodies were found. In one boy's stomach was his last meal: Kentucky Fried Chicken.

Edmund Kemper's confession was taken as a joke.

Edmund Kemper committed his first murder at age fifteen, shooting and killing his grandparents in 1964. After serving a five-year prison sentence, he dismembered, murdered, and then had sex with two Fresno State University students. He murdered four more women, then his mother and her best friend, before fleeing. Shortly after, he telephoned police to turn himself in, confess his crimes, and say that he would be "happy going about his life in prison." They thought it was a prank call, so he had to show up in person to turn himself in.

Edmund Kemper's sister tried to kill him on two occasions.

Edmund Kemper survived two childhood murder attempts at the hands of his sister, Susan, which supports the theory that the urge to kill may be hereditary, or at least linked to children of the same parents growing up in the same damaging environment. She once tried to push him in front of a speeding train. She also threw him into the deep end of a pool knowing he couldn't swim.

Randy Kraft's meticulous note-taking got him convicted.

Randy Kraft murdered primarily hitchhikers with military backgrounds in the 1970s and 1980s. His killing ground spanned Oregon, California, and Michigan. In 1983, he was arrested by the California Highway Patrol, who immediately spotted some fairly damning evidence: a dead body sitting in the passenger seat. A further investigation of the car turned up a briefcase that contained Kraft's diary full of detailed notes on the deaths of sixty people. He was ultimately convicted of sixteen murders.

Randy Kraft claimed his murder journal was a party invite list.

One of the most damning pieces of evidence used against Randy Kraft was a "scorecard" he kept, seemingly of his murders. Through a series of codes, Kraft kept very detailed notes about exactly how he tortured and killed as many as sixty-one victims. Investigators found that forty-three entries lined up perfectly with the circumstances of specific murders; Kraft claimed that the list was actually a coded journal of his sexual conquests. Then he later said it was a list of housewarming party invites for his boyfriend.

Four famous serial killers became friends behind bars.

In 1989, San Quentin State Prison in California was the home of four captured and convicted serial killers: Lawrence Bittaker, William Boni, Randy Kraft, and Douglas Clark. Together, they formed what they called the San Quentin Bridge Club. Every day they got together and played cards.

Police officers loved Edmund Kemper.

When his crimes were being investigated, Edmund Kemper befriended the detectives on the case. He figured out that they frequented a cop bar called the Jury Room, and became such a fixture there that they openly discussed the case with him. After he turned himself in, the police were shocked that "Big Ed," all friendly and jovial, was the same person as the evil "Coed Killer."

One serial killer thought his murders prevented earthquakes.

Herbert Mullin, who was active as a serial killer in Santa Cruz, California, around the same time as Edmund Kemper (1972–73), murdered thirteen people. Once captured, he readily confessed to the killings, proudly taking credit because doing so had prevented massive earthquakes from devastating California, or so he believed.

The statistics on American serial killers are chilling.

Since the 1980s, there have been 222,000 unsolved serial killer murders in the U.S. Serial killer killings in California are the highest in the U.S. at 1,682. Seventy percent of all known serial killer murders happen in America.

There are four categories of serial killer motives.

Criminal psychologists say serial killers have one of four motivations. Some are mission-oriented and bent on cleansing society or ridding the world of filth. Some are hedonists who derive pleasure from killing. Then there are visionary murderers, compelled to kill by Satan or God. And finally, there are the power-hungry killers who do it for control.

Numbers define serial killing.

Per the FBI's definition, a serial killer is someone who has killed three or more people in a repeated fashion. That excludes some repeat murderers like the Canadian couple Paul Bernardo and Karla Homolka. They are not technically serial killers under this definition because while they killed three people, one of those was classified as manslaughter.

Serial killers often share a similar biological profile.

Around 24 percent of psychopaths show abnormal EEG brain wave patterns. As many as 55 percent of serial killers suffered a traumatic brain injury as a child or adolescent, with some sustaining damage to the prefrontal cortex, where planning and judgment occur. Half of serial killers have personality disorders.

It's extremely rare to be murdered by a serial killer.

According the FBI, about 15,000 people are murdered in the U.S. each year. Of that number, about 1 percent, or 150, are attributable to the twenty or so active serial killers at any given time. Based on those figures, you've got a 0.00039 percent chance of being a serial killer's victim.

A serial killer in India was frighteningly young.

The youngest convicted serial killer on record is eight-year-old Amarjeet Sada. He confessed to murdering the missing babies in his village in India, including a sister and a cousin. His parents knew but remained silent; in 2007, he revealed the burial sites when questioned by police. Trying a child as an adult is illegal in India, so the longest sentence he could get was three years in a juvenile facility.

Serial killers are almost never old.

It's rare for serial killers to kill past the age of fifty-five, and unheard of to start that old. That makes Canadian Bruce McArthur the oldest serial killer. He started killing after age sixty, murdering eight men in total.

Killer Jerry Brudos kept grisly proof of his murders.

While most serial killers dispose of the remains of those they've killed right away—to avoid detection or to eliminate evidence— some keep a souvenir of their killings. Jerry Brudos, an Oregon-based serial killer in the 1960s, chopped off the feet of one of his victims and placed them on his mantel—a trophy of his accomplishment.

Ted Bundy wrote what he knew.

After being sentenced to live out his days on Florida's death row in the early 1980s, serial killer Ted Bundy helped authorities in another state track down another serial killer. The bodies of women started to wash up in the Green River near Seattle, and police were stumped as to the identity of their murderer. Bundy put together a psychological profile of the suspect. The FBI also made a psych profile, but Bundy's was more effective in that it helped lead them to capture their murderer, Gary Ridgway.

Ted Bundy killed in Florida because he thought that would get him executed.

Serial killer Ted Bundy killed in many states, but he may have wanted someone to kill him. In 1976, in conversation with a lawyer in Colorado, he learned that Florida was the top state for executions. So, when he was released from prison, he moved to Florida, killed again, and that's where he was executed in 1989.

Ted Bundy easily escaped prison.

After escaping from and eluding police, Ted Bundy returned to custody in 1977. A judge ordered that the serial killer wear ankle shackles during hearings; he'd previously escaped from the Pitkin County Courthouse. The judge had let him visit the law library unshackled (so he could better represent himself), and he jumped out of a second-story window. Prison officials also arranged for a welder to install extra bars in Bundy's cell to prevent him from escaping again. The welder never showed up, and Bundy did escape again.

Ted Bundy performed many good deeds.

Apparently, he wasn't totally evil. Ted Bundy once saved a drowning toddler, stopped an accused purse snatcher by tackling him, and served as assistant director of Seattle's Crime Prevention Advisory Commission, all before his first murder. After he started killing, he worked at a suicide prevention hotline.

Ted Bundy could have killed Debbie Harry.

In the early 1970s, before she was the lead singer of Blondie, Debbie Harry was trying to get a ride to a club at about 4 A.M. A white car pulled up, and the driver offered her a ride as she tried to hail a cab. He was persistent, so she gave in and got into the VW Beetle. She immediately had a bad feeling: The interior of the car was stripped down, and the doors had no handles and no way of getting out from the inside. She kept rolling down the window ever so slowly until she could open the door from the outside. The driver noticed, turned a corner fast, and she tumbled out as she opened the door, hitting the middle of the street. That driver: Ted Bundy.

Ted Bundy skipped his last meal.

Ted Bundy didn't order a fancy last meal before he was executed in Florida in 1989. He was given the standard death row last meal: a cheap steak and eggs. He didn't eat it, so a guard gobbled it down after Bundy's execution.

Charles Manson called Ted Bundy names.

After Ted Bundy was executed in 1989 for his serial murders, Charles Manson released a public statement expressing his disdain for the killer, thoughts he'd previously made known privately and to reporters. "Bundy's a rumpkin. Bundy's a poop butt. Bundy's his mama's boy. Bundy's out there trying to prove something to his own manhood. That's got nothin' to do with me," Manson declared. "I don't roll around with poop people like that."

A rival inmate severely burned Charles Manson.

While serving out his life sentence in a California prison in 1984, Charles Manson was nearly killed by another inmate named Jan Holmstrom. Holmstrom claimed that Manson had threatened to kill him because of his interest in the Hare Krishna religion, and he retaliated by dousing Manson in paint thinner and setting him aflame. Manson was seriously burned over 20 percent of his body, particularly on his hands, face, and scalp. He would have been more seriously burned had his beard not protected his face.

The Boston Strangler tried to make himself look like a burglar, but he didn't steal anything.

The Boston Strangler left thirteen women, with ages ranging from nineteen to eighty-five, in his wake when he started his killings in 1964. The culprit made every murder scene look like a burglary to throw police off, but it only raised suspicion because nothing ever seemed to be missing. When Albert DeSalvo was arrested for his role in the "Green Man" rapes, he admitted everything. In 1973, while serving time, he was stabbed to death by a fellow inmate.

Postmortem DNA testing proved the identity of the Boston Strangler.

While prosecutors acted on Albert DeSalvo's admission that he was the Boston Strangler, there remained some inconsistencies in his story that made them doubt him. In fact, numerous DNA analysis attempts in the 1990s and 2000s couldn't connect DeSalvo to the crimes. In 2013, scientists isolated the DNA from a semen sample left on one of the victims and tested it against a sample provided by DeSalvo's nephew. It was a familial match, indicating in overwhelming certainty that DeSalvo could've been the murderer. A judge ordered DeSalvo's body exhumed, and after testing the body, it was confirmed as a DNA match.

Ottis Toole was one sauce away from cannibalism.

Starting in the 1970s, Ottis Toole and Henry Lee Lucas traversed the country killing people indiscriminately and, when it came to Lucas, doing away with the evidence by eating the victims. He'd dismember them and grill them on a barbecue, but Toole never joined in. When authorities later asked Toole why he hadn't cannibalized them, he explained, "Because I don't like barbecue sauce."

Albert Fish's use of a particular envelope ended his horrible crime spree.

Albert Fish had a lot of nicknames before his identification and capture, including "the Brooklyn Vampire" and "the Gray Man." He kidnapped children by befriending their parents, then raped them, murdered them, and ate their bodies. He killed as many as a hundred people but only ever confessed to three. He was arrested (and executed) in 1936, but only because he sent a letter to the mother of one of his youngest victims, detailing exactly how he killed her and what parts of her he ate. He sent the note in an envelope with a recognizable emblem that he had picked up at his boardinghouse. It was easily traced back to Fish.

Albert Fish endured a lot of pain, mostly because he enjoyed it.

Albert Fish went through the process of death via the electric chair twice, because the first blast of electricity didn't kill him. That's because an excessive amount of metal in his body prevented the electricity from spreading quickly. He was a sadomasochist who pushed needles into his skin and genitals for gratification. A postmortem X-ray uncovered twenty-seven needles alone in his pelvic region.

Australian police caught a serial killer who literally took their bait.

Eric Edgar Cooke was found responsible for twenty-two violent crimes, including eight deaths, in Perth, Australia, from 1958 to 1963. He was eventually put to death by hanging. Perth police captured Cooke in a novel, almost cartoonish way. After finding a rifle he'd discarded in a row of bushes, police replaced it with a similar gun and tied it to a length of fishing line. And then they waited, staking out the location for seventeen days until Cooke went to retrieve his firearm, and the tug on the fishing line alerted authorities.

A Canadian killer copied *Dexter*.

The hit cable show *Dexter* centered around a conflicted serial killer who satisfied his bloodlust by only killing other serial killers. Canadian filmmaker Mark Twitchell wrote on his Facebook profile in 2008 that he has "way too much in common with Dexter Morgan." Later that year, he answered Johnny Altinger's personal ad that he'd placed in an Edmonton newspaper. Twitchell answered the ad and showed up at Altinger's place pretending to be a woman so he'd let him in. Altinger's body was never found, but Twitchell was arrested and sentenced to life in prison after police found a detailed, pointed murder plan stating how he planned to kill him. It was all taken from *Dexter*.

Bobby Joe Long said his victims wanted to be dead.

Bobby Joe Long claimed to be acting on orders from God to kill, which meant only killing certain women, the ones who told him they wanted to be killed. Long claimed that all of his victims had communicated with him telepathically to let him know they were ready to be a sacrifice.

The Hillside Strangler was actually two Hillside Stranglers.

The Hillside Strangler turned out to be two men, cousins Kenneth Bianchi and Angelo Buono. They killed ten girls and women in Los Angeles, but Bianchi tried to avoid the death penalty by pleading not guilty by reason of insanity. Mental health professionals observed him and reported that he was doing a poor job of faking multiple personality disorder. When he became aware of their assessment, Buono changed his plea to guilty and testified against his cousin to cut himself a better deal.

One of the Hillside Stranglers helped investigate the Hillside Strangler case.

While one half of the duo operated as the Hillside Strangler, Kenneth Bianchi started the process of joining the Los Angeles Police Department. As part of his pre-academy enrollment training, he participated in multiple police ride-alongs, all while investigators were looking for the Hillside Strangler.

The Hillside Stranglers left a Hollywood scion alone.

Angelo Buono and Kenneth Bianchi approached a woman in 1977, thinking she looked like classic creepy movie actor Peter Lorre. Catherine Lorre confirmed that she was the actor's daughter, and the two men who would combine efforts to be known as the Hillside Strangler left her alone, partly because they were fans of Lorre and partly because they didn't want to invite attention by killing a celebrity's daughter.

The scene of the West murders was absolutely destroyed.

Between 1967 and 1987, Fred and Rosemary West killed twelve young women at their home in Gloucester, England, nicknamed "the House of Horrors" by the British press. After sexually abusing the women, the Wests murdered their victims, dismembered the bodies, and buried the remains in their garden or cellar. To discourage people from taking souvenirs, the home where Fred and Rosemary West killed these women was demolished. After that, every brick was crushed and every piece of wood burned, leaving nothing behind.

The Wests' daughter later realized a creepy fact about her childhood.

Mae West (not the actress), the daughter of serial killers Fred and Rosemary West, played dress-up as a child using whatever clothing she found around the house. She had no idea then, but when she grew up, it dawned on her that the clothes were belongings of her parents' victims.

Charles Manson died a wealthy man.

While not legally permitted to profit from his crimes or use his image in a commercial manner, Charles Manson sold paintings, T-shirts, photos, and interviews through websites operated by associates. He couldn't access the money, but he earned it nonetheless.

Job offers were really an invitation to murder on a San Francisco torture ranch.

In the 1950s and 1960s, Delfina and Maria de Jesus Gonzalez ran a Mexican prostitution ring near San Francisco known as Las Poquianchis. They recruited by placing ads for nonexistent jobs in newspapers, and when women showed up for the jobs, they were taken by force to their ranch, tortured, sold into sexual slavery, and then murdered once their clients found them no longer desirable. When a victim escaped, the authorities tracked down and captured the killers and found the remains of eighty women, eleven men, and several fetuses.

A famous ad slogan was inspired by the last words of a killer.

The Wieden + Kennedy ad agency launched Nike's proactive "Just Do It" campaign in 1988. It was inspired in part by the words of Gary Gilmore, who was executed in 1977 for murdering two people in Utah in 1976. When he faced a five-man firing squad, his final statement was, "Let's do it." Wieden remembered Gilmore's last words when trying to come up with the Nike slogan, and used it as the foundation for the now-famous brand slogan.

Only one serial killer has been linked to Delaware.

From 1987 to 1988, several prostitutes along Route 40 in Delaware were picked up and then murdered. The only bit of conclusive linking evidence that police could find were blue carpet fibers on some of the bodies. An undercover police officer posed as a prostitute and was approached by Steven Brian Pennell, who was driving an electrician's van—lined with blue carpeting. The officer brushed the carpet playfully with her hand and pulled a few fibers from it before refusing a ride. Another officer ran the plates on the van. This evidence would ultimately help lead to his conviction.

Bullet fragments in an attempted murder led police to a serial killer.

Christine Smith was hired for sex by a man in 1998, but when he couldn't perform, he became enraged and attacked her. In the struggle, he pulled out a gun and shot her. The bullet grazed her head. She escaped, was hospitalized for a head wound that she had thought was from a knife, and reported the attack to police. A few years later, she had X-rays after a car accident, and they showed bullet fragments lodged in her skull. The fragments were extracted, matched, and identified as similar to those of a .25 caliber gun registered to serial killer Robert Lee Yates.

Ed Gein didn't submit to a full trial.

There existed a preponderance of evidence against Ed Gein, who stole body parts from cemeteries near his Wisconsin hometown and also murdered two people to obtain the raw materials he needed to make housewares and clothing. But in 1968, he was only officially tried for one murder to keep down the cost of the courtroom trial because his Wisconsin jurisdiction was so cash-strapped at the time.

Ed Gein repurposed the remains of his murder victims.

Ed Gein didn't dispose of his victims' bodies; he utilized them. Gein had skulls on his bedposts, a bowl made from a skull, leggings made from leg skin, masks made from facial skin, and according to police who found it, a heart sitting in a bag on his stove.

A teenage serial killer nearly gained access to a large group of children.

Future serial killer Scott Thomas Erskine, as a teenager, beat a fourteen-year-old boy nearly to death during a rape attempt gone awry. It was the summer of 1980, and he was on his way to interview for a job to be a teenage camp counselor.

A serial killer infiltrated his own investigation.

A man named Captain Marcel Valeri serving with the Paris Police Department was considered such a good detective that he was assigned to track down killer Marcel Petiot, who was wanted for nearly two dozen murders in the 1940s. Then someone in a Paris metro station recognized Valeri. Without the long beard he had grown, it was clear he was Marcel Petiot.

A serial killer murdered a man for a crime he'd later commit.

Tommy Lynn Sells was believed to be the murderer responsible for the deaths of seventy people, for which he was executed in 2014. He also raped children; the victim that got him the death penalty was thirteen. This was darkly ironic, because his first murder occurred at age sixteen, when he killed a man who was in the act of molesting a child.

A kidnapping victim used religion to gain her freedom.

Wanted by police for the murder of Carrie Marie Scott, the latest murder in a string that began in 1971, Steven Morin went on the lam in 1981. On the road, he kidnapped a woman named Margaret Palm, who rode with Morin for ten hours. Determined to survive, she used religion to soften her abductor, making him listen to tapes of televangelist Kenneth Copeland and reading aloud her favorite Bible verses from her journal. Morin released Palm, and told her that he was going to turn himself in to Copeland personally when he got to Texas, but he was arrested before he could.

Sean Vincent Gillis had a sick sense of humor.

From 1994 to 2004, Sean Vincent Gillis stalked, assaulted, murdered, and defiled the corpses of eight women in the Baton Rouge, Louisiana, area. His first victim was found abandoned on the side of a street, placed under a "Dead End" road sign. Gillis would later admit that he'd purposely placed the body there as a dark joke.

A TV crime show ended a serial killer's final spree.

Kenneth McDuff received a lot of second chances, and he didn't take any of them. Sentenced to three simultaneous death sentences for his murders, he wound up paroled and released in 1989. Three days later, he killed a woman. But what sent him back to prison was a parole violation for making death threats. Amazingly, he was paroled again in 1990, started murdering again in 1991, and killed five people in total by 1992, when he was arrested after a coworker saw his case profiled on *America's Most Wanted*.

The serial killer who killed the most was only convicted for a few murders.

The most prolific serial killer in American history is likely Samuel Little. While he claims to have killed a total of ninety-three women between 1970 and 2005, the FBI has confirmed his role in the deaths of sixty of the victims (so far), the largest number of murder victims in U.S. history. He was sentenced to life without parole for just four of those murders.

A Buffalo serial murderer's crimes started after he tried to commit himself.

In the early 1980s, Joseph Christopher killed twelve people in and around Buffalo, with another seven surviving his attacks. His murders were largely carried out with point-blank shooting of a .22 caliber sawed-off shotgun, earning him the nickname "the .22 Caliber Killer." All his murder victims were Black, and Christopher's killings were racially motivated. Mere weeks before the killing spree began, Christopher knew he didn't feel right. His urge to kill prompted him to try and admit himself to the Buffalo Psychiatric Center, but he was turned away.

Homophobia in the 1970s allowed a San Francisco serial killer to walk free.

In the 1970s, a serial killer nicknamed "the Doodler" targeted gay men in the San Francisco area. He had a habit of drawing portraits of his male victims in the nude before he killed them. Three men who posed for the drawings survived the attack, but wouldn't testify as to his identity in court out of fear of publicly outing themselves as homosexuals.

A hospital orderly discovered his passion for murder accidentally.

Donald Harvey worked as an orderly in Ohio and Kentucky hospitals in the 1970s and 1980s. He killed a confirmed thirty-seven patients, though according to him the number is closer to seventy. The hospital was a good place for him to hide being a bringer of death, and it's also how he started killing. His first death was an accident: He connected a patient to an empty oxygen tank, the person died, and he kept killing because he liked the feeling of taking a life.

A brutal death sentence in Pakistan was never actually carried out.

In 2001, Javed Iqbal of Pakistan received one of the most lurid and creative death sentences of all time. He was set to be cut into one hundred pieces, then placed into a vat of acid to dissolve. That's the way he killed more than one hundred boys and teenagers. But Iqbal didn't die that way. Instead, he died by suicide in his prison cell before the execution.

A trail of peas led police to a serial killer.

In what is now Germany, sixteenth-century bandit Christman Genipperteinga was also a shockingly prolific serial killer, ending the life of 964 people over a period of thirteen years. Six of those deaths were of his own children, born to a woman he kidnapped and held as a sex slave for seven years. He was caught when the woman was allowed to go into town, and then dropped a trail of peas for authorities to follow back to Genipperteinga's lair.

Kurt Vonnegut's daughter made an early connection between two murderers.

Paul John Knowles killed eighteen people across multiple states in 1974, with a possible body count as high as thirty-five. Because he was suave and handsome (and because he targeted women), the media nicknamed him "the Casanova Killer." After his crimes came to light and he was arrested, Edith Vonnegut, daughter of acclaimed writer Kurt Vonnegut, claimed to have known him in the 1960s, and she had, in that decade, compared him to Charles Manson before anyone knew that both men would become murderers.

Nobody was convinced by any of Marty Graham's explanations for the dead bodies in his apartment.

Harrison "Marty" Graham changed his story a lot. In August 1987, he was evicted for an overwhelmingly foul odor coming from his apartment, which, upon police investigation, turned out to be the decomposing bodies of seven women hidden throughout the home. Graham at first said he knew they were there, because they'd been there when he moved in. Then he said that all of the women had died when he accidentally strangled them during sex.

Marty Graham desperately loved Cookie Monster.

Harrison "Marty" Graham was convicted and imprisoned for his seven murders, for which police found to be no accident. The worst part for Graham about being taken into police custody was that he was permanently separated from a Cookie Monster doll he had the habit of taking everywhere. He slept with the doll and had intimate conversations with it, but it was seized as evidence and never returned.

Two serial killers' wives thought they were cheating, not murdering.

Robert Lee Yates and Gary Ridgway were both serial killers who were active in the 1980s and 90s. They didn't know each other, but they had one thing in common. During their serial killing days, both men were married to wives who became suspicious of their husbands' sketchy whereabouts and nighttime activities. Both figured their husbands were carrying on an extramarital affair. The possibility that they were serial killers never occurred to either man's wife.

There's a serial killer who saved the life of another serial killer.

Kenneth Erskine was sentenced to prison for his multiple murders—murders that earned him the nickname "the Stockwell Strangler." In 1981, Peter Sutcliffe, a.k.a. the Yorkshire Ripper, was arrested, prosecuted, and sent to prison, where he was attacked by another inmate and nearly strangled to death. Weirdly enough, it was Erskine, a serial strangler, who pulled the assailant off him and saved Sutcliffe's life.

Prisoners kept trying to kill the Yorkshire Ripper.

Peter Sutcliffe, known as the Yorkshire Ripper because eleven of the thirteen murders he committed against women occurred in the English region of West Yorkshire, was sent to prison to serve out his concurrent life sentences. Behind bars, he survived numerous attempts on his life by other inmates. In 1983, James Costello slashed Sutcliffe's face with broken glass. In 1999, Paul Wilson strangled Sutcliffe with a pair of headphones, but was pulled off by two other prisoners. In 2000, Ian McKay stabbed Sutcliffe with a pen in both eyes, blinding him in one. And in 2011, Patrick Sureda tried to remove Sutcliffe's remaining good eye with a knife.

The 1970s and 1980s were the peak of serial killing.

In the 1970s and 1980s, there were so many serial killers operating in the U.S. that they were responsible for about 400 deaths. Due to advances in criminology, mental health, psychology, law enforcement, and surveillance technology, that number dropped to sixty-one in the first decade of the twenty-first century.

Truck stops were the key to catching more serial killers.

Law enforcement programs pinpointing and busting serial killers have been especially effective in curbing crime. The FBI established the Highway Serial Killings Initiative. So many bodies have been discovered at or near highway truck stops, and so many deaths attributed to cross-country truck drivers, that the FBI started to target the places where anonymity and quick stops are a matter of course. More than thirty old murder cases have been solved by investigating truck stops.

Some states are more likely to harbor serial killers.

Broken out into a state-by-state basis, some jurisdictions seem to yield more serial killers than others. The southwestern United States is where the most serial killings occur, but on a per capita basis, Alaska is the deadliest for serial killings—sixteen deaths per one million residents. A total of fifty-one murders by serial killers have happened in the far northern state, with more than half of those coming in the 1980s and 1990s. Most of the other half was the work of one man, Robert Hansen, who was originally from Iowa but moved to Alaska. He would kidnap women, set them loose on his land, and hunt them like animals for sport.

There are six parts of the serial killer cycle.

Criminal psychologists have broken down the serial killer cycle into six distinct parts. 1: Aura phase, in which the killer loses touch with reality. 2: Trolling phase, or searching for a victim. 3: Wooing, or luring in a victim. 4: Capturing the victim. 5: The murder itself. 6: Post-murder depression, which resolves with the cycle beginning anew.

The internet spawned its first serial murderer in the early 1990s.

The first serial killer of the internet age, meaning the first one to use online resources to find his victims, was John E. Robinson. In 1993, he was released from prison after serving time for running a prostitution ring. He then used the nascent internet, namely its chat rooms, where he posted under the name "Slavemaster" to charm women into coming to his home for sex and then killing them.

There are warning signs in children who might grow up to be serial killers.

Serial killers can't be predicted, but most share similar warning signs of what's to come. If they torture animals as children, wet the bed past the age of twelve, and exhibit symptoms of pyromania, or starting fires, that's a red flag. According to criminologists, the shorthand for this is "the Triad."

Serial killers aren't any smarter than the rest of the population.

An analysis of the intellect levels of serial killers found no correlation between the desire to murder and mental aptitude. Most have perfectly average IQs, but there are a few notable exceptions. Serial bombers, or those who repeatedly kill with explosives, tend to have a significantly higher intellect than that of the general public.

Doctors can be serial killers, too.

British doctor Harold Shipman, a children's asthma specialist, was convicted of killing fifteen people, but he may have killed up to 250 people. His mode of murder: He would diagnose patients with false illnesses, then inject them with a lethal dose of diamorphine.

One old serial killer's diary sent him to prison.

Joseph Naso was seventy-six years old and on parole for robbing a grocery store when police investigated his Reno, Nevada, home to do a routine check as outlined in the terms of his release. While looking for forbidden items like guns and drugs, a police officer uncovered a large amount of women's clothing (Naso lived alone) alongside mannequin parts, and hundreds of photos of naked, unconscious women. Finally, the officer found a journal that detailed Naso's many crimes dating back decades. The diary linked Naso to four previously unsolved murders of women that occurred between 1977 and 1994.

Richard Chase was a serial killer and a vampire.

Sacramento-based serial killer Richard Chase believed himself to be a vampire. Over a period of one month, he killed six people and gave in to the urge to drink their blood. Because vampire lore requires vampires to be invited into a residence before they can enter, Chase chose his victims by entering the homes of strangers who had left their doors unlocked. He considered that as good as an invitation.

Jake Bird admitted to killing other people, in an odd aim to delay his execution.

Just before his 1948 execution for the ax murder of Bertha Kludt and her daughter, Jake Bird told police and prosecutors that he'd killed forty-four other people and could help them close those cases. He knew that authorities would have to investigate his claims and that it would prolong his life. His ploy worked, but he was eventually hanged for Kludt's murder in 1949.

The Unabomber was once thought to also be the Zodiac Killer.

After the arrest of Ted Kaczynski in 1996, when he was proved to be the Unabomber, deliverer of remote mail bombs, investigators in San Francisco entertained the idea that he was also the similarly once anonymous Zodiac Killer. At the time of the murders in 1968–69, Kaczynski resembled the composite sketch and had similar handwriting, and both used a complex code of ciphers, Kaczynski in his diary and the Zodiac Killer in his notes to police. Fingerprint samples ultimately ruled out the possibility that the Unabomber was also the Zodiac Killer.

A lifesaving arsonist went on to kill more than a dozen people.

In October 1971, Arthur Shawcross was released from prison after serving twenty-two months of a five-year prison sentence for arson. He was sprung as a reward for saving the life of a guard during a riot. Within a year of being granted freedom, Shawcross had assaulted and murdered two children, and was back in prison with a twenty-five-year term. Halfway through, he was paroled, and declared rehabilitated. Then he killed eleven more people.

Frank Sinatra and Muhammad Ali tried to help catch an Atlanta child murderer.

Tracking down the culprit responsible for the Atlanta child murders in the 1980s was so expensive for the cash-strapped Georgia metropolis that it lost the city huge sums of money. In 1981, Mayor Maynard Jackson invited Frank Sinatra and Sammy Davis Jr. to perform a benefit concert to fund the search, and to get the city out of debt. The event raised $200,000, of which Jackson promised half to anyone who cracked the case and ended the killing spree. A month after Muhammad Ali donated $400,000 to the reward fund, Wayne Williams was arrested and prosecuted. (He didn't get the reward.)

One serial killer got rid of his victims by turning them into livestock feed.

Robert Pickton was arrested in 2002 and became known as "the Pig Farmer Killer," a nickname that referred to the man's practice of feeding the remains of his murder victims to his hungry pigs. To get a confession, authorities sent a police officer into his holding cell with an undercover cop pretending to be another offender. Pickton confessed to forty-nine murders, expressing disappointment that he never made it to "the big five-O" on account of his being "sloppy."

Some Amazon product reviews conclusively linked a serial killer to his crimes.

Police were able to link Todd Kohlhepp to a series of murders because of his brutally honest—to the point of confessional—Amazon product reviews. From 2014 to 2016, Kohlhepp offered his two cents on stuff he used as murder gear, including knives, gun accessories, targets, and tactical equipment. "Keep in car for when you have to hide the bodies and you left the full-size shovel at home," he wrote about a folding shovel. The reviews lined up with the timing of his latest murders and linked to a wish list under the killer's real name.

The wife of a serial killer made a fortune for her husband's confessions.

In 1981, Clifford Olson was caught by police and identified as the murderer of eleven children and young adults in British Columbia. He agreed to confess to get his trial going, but for a steep price: In exchange for revealing the whereabouts of the remains of each body, his wife would receive $10,000 paid into a trust fund. Mrs. Olson thusly received $100,000 (because the eleventh victim's resting place was a free bonus from Olson).

One serial killer's victims helped execute him.

Families of the victims of Mohammed Bijeh got to participate in his execution. In March 2005, Bijeh was put to death by the government of Iran for his serial killing. After he was lashed one hundred times, a mob of 5,000 tried to rush the gallows. Riot police held them back, but a brother of one of Bijeh's victims got through and stabbed the killer in the back. Then the mother of another victim personally placed the noose around his neck, and then he was hanged from a crane until he was dead.

Serial killer Pee-Wee Gaskins killed while he was locked up.

Donald "Pee-Wee" Gaskins, incarcerated on South Carolina's death row for twelve murders, managed to kill again while in prison, and his victim was another death row inmate. He had it in for Rudolph Tyner, unsuccessfully trying to off him by poisoning his food on multiple occasions. Finally, Gaskins made a fake portable radio out of plastic explosives and left it in Tyner's cell; the individual held the fake radio up to his ear at the time Gaskins had it rigged to explode.

There are probably murder victims buried underneath some of California's freeways.

From 1953 to 1970, Mack Ray Edwards kidnapped, sexually assaulted, and then murdered six children (at least that's how many have been confirmed) in the Los Angeles area. Edwards worked as a heavy equipment operator for CalTrans, the state agency responsible for building California's burgeoning freeway system in the 1950s, so he dumped his victims in areas he knew would soon be paved over. One victim's remains were found disposed in such a manner, and Edwards eventually admitted to burying other bodies in other freeway construction sites.

A Colombian killer received an impossibly long prison sentence.

Luis Alfredo Garavito, because of the sheer volume of his crimes, received a prison sentence of 1,853 years. That was quickly and significantly reduced when he agreed to help police find other burial sites of his victims, and was limited because of Colombian sentencing laws. He ultimately only served twenty-two years and was paroled in 2021.

Israel Keyes left a lengthy digital record for police.

Authorities have confirmed that Israel Keyes committed three murders, but he confessed to many more, along with arson, bank robberies, and sexual assaults. In 2012, he kidnapped, raped, and killed Samantha Koening. After she was dead, he pretended that she wasn't. He stole Koening's debit card and demanded a ransom of $30,000 transferred to the account in exchange for the woman's return. Surveillance video of Koening at ATMs in the Southwest made it easy for police to find him.

An IP address located a St. Louis killer.

A serial killer terrorized St. Louis from 2001 to 2002, with police theorizing in a local newspaper that the suspect had killed "up to nine women." The man purporting to be the murderer was incensed, wanting credit for having committed seventeen recent murders. He went so far as to include a map with an "X" marked where he'd buried his seventeenth victim. Police found the body, and then they found the serial killer, Maury Troy Travis, who'd used Expedia to print out the map. Expedia gave police his computer's IP address, and police were able to link it to his home address.

CHAPTER 3

Crimes of Passion

Murder is a planned act, but crimes
of passion are often tragedies that
occur in the moment, with little
forethought but plenty of intensity,
emotion, and dark urges playing a role.

One of the first school shootings occurred because of the "blahs."

Brenda Spencer lived across the street from Grover Cleveland Elementary School in suburban San Diego. One Monday morning in January 1979, as children and faculty arrived for classes, the sixteen-year-old aimed a rifle at the schoolyard and started firing. With the onslaught of bullets, Spencer killed the school's custodian and principal and injured eight children. Spencer was tried as an adult, entered a guilty plea, and received a life sentence. When asked by a reporter why she did what she did, Spencer coldly replied, "I just did it because it's a way to cheer the day up. Nobody likes Mondays." An Irish band called the Boomtown Rats wrote a song about the killings that they performed at Live Aid called "I Don't Like Mondays."

The man who caught Jeffrey Dahmer later killed a man.

Tracy Edwards survived a handcuffed, violent encounter in 1991 in Jeffrey Dahmer's apartment, and brought police to his assailant's home, where they discovered enough evidence to charge Dahmer with seventeen counts of murder. Twenty years and four days after he ended Dahmer's cannibalistic murder campaign, in July 2011, Edwards himself was arrested for murder. He was spotted on a bridge over the Milwaukee River with another guy (felon Timothy Carr) throwing a man named Jonny Jordan into the water, where he drowned. Evidently, this was the result of a fight. Edwards was sentenced to eighteen months in prison for aiding a felon.

One man was a veterinarian, professor, Olympic athlete, and murderer.

Dr. James Snook was a veterinary medicine professor at Ohio State University. He also invented a commonly used dog-spaying tool and won two gold medals in shooting events at the 1920 Olympics. In 1926, Snook took up with Theora Hix, a teenage OSU undergrad. One night in 1929, they went out for a drive together and got high. On that same excursion, he decided that he was done with Hix. He grabbed the hammer he kept in his car and smashed Hix in the head with it. Then he took out his pocket knife and slit Hix's throat. He was arrested, confessed, and died in the electric chair in 1930.

A reality show was canceled after a contestant committed a murder.

In 2009, VH1 debuted the dating show *Megan Wants a Millionaire*, in which Megan Hauserman of previous dating show *Rock of Love* chose a partner from a pool of seventeen rich men. VH1 canceled the show after three episodes and shelved the remaining installments after one of those rich guys, Ryan Jenkins, was the sole suspect in the murder of Jasmine Fiore, the woman he'd married right after filming finished on *Megan Wants a Millionaire*. Four days later, Jenkins (who finished in third place on the series) died by suicide in a British Columbia motel.

A twelve-year-old was convicted of murder in the 1990s.

In 1999, Curtis Fairchild Jones (and his sister, Catherine) shot and killed their father's girlfriend. Their lawyers argued that they had been abused by her, a charge that had been investigated by Florida child welfare agencies. The siblings were tried as adults and convicted of murder—even though Curtis and Catherine were just twelve and thirteen years old, respectively, at the time of the crime. Curtis Fairchild Jones is thus the youngest person ever convicted of murder in the United States. (He was released from prison in 2015.)

An eighty-five-year-old is the oldest convicted murderer of all time.

Leonard Sherman of Daly City, California, had worked out a deal with his sister, Betty Dreyfuss. He'd give her $75,000 in Treasury Bills in exchange for her paying the rent on their shared home, his medical costs, and other expenses he was struggling to pay. In July 1999, the deal soured. Sherman went into his sister's bedroom with two handguns and shot her dead. In part because Sherman showed no remorse, he was sentenced to two life sentences for murder via firearm. At eighty-five years old, he's the oldest convicted murderer in American history.

A killer bellhop didn't want to leave prison.

In 1911, a hotel bellhop named Paul Geidel snuck into the room occupied by William H. Jackson, a retired Wall Street stockbroker. Looking to steal the large amounts of cash Jackson reportedly kept in his room, Geidel suffocated the sleeping man with a chloroform-soaked rag. But the rumors weren't true. Geidel made off with just $7 and was arrested that same day. He was sentenced to twenty years to life in jail. Geidel was paroled in 1974 after sixty-three years of time served, but he didn't want to leave prison. Officials finally convinced him to leave in 1980, and with sixty-nine years behind bars, that's the longest stint ever in the American prison system.

A murder-suicide ended up just being a suicide.

Donald Sexton was ordered to stay away from his estranged wife, Tammy Sexton, for six months, following a domestic violence charge. In 2009, a week into the order, Donald went to Tammy's home while she slept, shot her in the head, then went outside and shot himself. Donald died. Tammy didn't. When police responded to her call, she was drinking a cup of tea and had a rag around her head to stanch the bleeding. Tests revealed that the bullet had entered and exited the middle of her head and passed through her brain without leaving any damage.

Too much sugar led to the death of Harvey Milk.

Harvey Milk was one of the first openly gay people elected to office in the U.S. He served on San Francisco's board of city supervisors in the 1970s. Milk actively campaigned for rights for LGBT citizens and passed equality legislation against the wishes of fellow supervisor Dan White, a conservative ex–police officer and the only board member who voted against Milk's bill. White resigned from the board after the passage, and after trying to get reinstated was so incensed that he went to city hall in November 1978 and shot and killed Milk (along with Mayor George Moscone). White's defense was that he'd eaten too much junk food, and all that sugar had left him mentally unstable. The first-degree murder charge was knocked down to manslaughter. White served just seven years in prison.

One killer asked for his sentence to match an athlete's jersey number.

Eric Torpy is a huge fan of NBA legend Larry Bird, so much so that in 2005, when a judge sentenced him to thirty years in prison for armed robbery and attempted murder, Torpy requested that his punishment be upped to thirty-three years—to match Bird's jersey number. The request was granted, but after a few years behind bars, Torpy petitioned the court to reinstate the thirty-year sentence. The request was denied; Torpy is eligible for parole in, coincidentally, 2033.

A convicted killer got married in the same courtroom where he was sentenced.

In 2013, Danne Desbrow went on trial for first-degree murder for a decade-old death, and despite arguing self-defense, he was found guilty. The high-profile trial took place over two months. It aroused the attention of Destiny Winters, Desbrow's high school sweetheart who had gotten pregnant at sixteen with Desbrow's son and wanted him to finally meet his father. The two rekindled their romance, and before his final sentencing, Desbrow proposed. Moments after Judge Patricia Cookson sentenced the groom to life in prison, she officiated the couple's courtroom wedding. She even baked a cake for the couple.

A deathbed confession led to more prison time.

James Washington, who was serving a fifteen-year sentence in a Tennessee prison for another crime, confessed to an unsolved murder from 1995 while on his deathbed due to a serious heart attack in 2009. However, against all odds, he recovered. As a result of his confession, his original fifteen-year sentence was increased to life in prison.

A motorcycle gang tried to kill Mick Jagger.

The Rolling Stones played a free concert at the Altamont
Speedway in California in December 1969, hiring members of the
Hells Angels biker gang to work security. They attacked and killed
a fan named Meredith Hunter; the Stones weren't aware of this
until after the show. The band promptly publicly denounced the
gang's behavior and bad-mouthed them, leading the Hells Angels
to hatch a revenge plot. They planned to invade Jagger's home in
Long Island, New York—arriving by boat—and then kill the singer.
A storm broke out when they were on their way, the boat
capsized, and they canceled the murder.

A scientist killed another scientist over a mess.

Annie Le was murdered on the day she was supposed to get
married in September 2009. Her body was discovered hidden
inside a wall in a laboratory at Yale University. Raymond Clark III,
who shared lab space with her, was arrested for the murder. He
was known to be a control freak and would get angry about the
perceived disorganization in the lab. It was believed that he choked
Le to death because her lab was too messy for his liking.

A woman awoke from a long coma and identified her attacker.

In June 2020, an unknown assailant attacked Wanda Palmer inside her home in Cottageville, West Virginia. She was so severely wounded by an ax that police believed she was dead when they responded to the call—the attempted murderer probably thought so, too. But she was breathing, and they brought her to a hospital. In July 2022, Palmer awoke from a two-year coma and gave the police the only lead they needed: Her brother, Daniel Palmer, had attacked her.

A murderer felt obligated to kill a fellow inmate.

The U.K. abolished the death penalty in 1969, but convicted killer Sidonio Teixeira still died suddenly and violently behind bars in 2016. He was serving a life sentence for murdering his three-year-old daughter, and he did his time at a Midlands prison at the same time as Victor Castigador, who was serving a life sentence in prison for two murders. He added a third to his rap sheet when he sneaked in a large rock, concealed it in a sock, and beat Teixeira to death with it. A former member of a criminal liquidation squad in his native Philippines, Castigador told police, "I'm wrong to kill somebody, but it's my job. Sometimes you have to punish evil."

The Boston Strangler was stabbed to death in prison.

People who have committed fewer murders than Albert DeSalvo have received the death penalty and have been executed for their crimes, which speaks to the vagaries and geographical discrepancies in the legal system. DeSalvo confessed to being the Boston Strangler in the 1960s, which linked him to the murders of thirteen women. But he was never convicted of murder, though he served a long sentence for multiple rapes. Nevertheless, DeSalvo died in prison after he was stabbed by a fellow inmate in 1973.

A robber defending himself made a critical, ridiculous error.

Dennis Newton went before an Oklahoma district court in 1985 on charges related to the armed robbery of a convenience store. Unhappy with his lawyer's actions, Newton released him and decided to act as his own defense attorney. By all accounts, the untrained lawyer managed to do a respectable job at defending himself, until the manager of the robbed store pinpointed Newton as the man who forcefully stole from his establishment. Newton, incensed, stood up and shouted, "I should have blown your head off!" Then he paused, and said, "If I'd been the one that was there." After just twenty minutes of deliberations, the jury convicted Newton and recommended a thirty-year prison term.

A car thief accidentally found himself on death row.

In December 1981, Nick Yarris and a friend stole a car while under the influence of drugs and alcohol in Delaware County, Pennsylvania, and were stopped by police. Yarris got into an altercation with the arresting officer, and the policeman's gun went off. This led to charges of attempted murder of a police officer. He was later acquitted of those charges, but in a misguided attempt to reduce his sentence for the car theft charge, he offered up information about the recent murder of a young mother. Yarris didn't kill her, but he said he had info on who did. His info didn't hold up, which turned suspicion on Yarris. He was convicted of the murder of Linda Mae Craig and spent twenty-three years on Delaware's death row before he was cleared by DNA evidence.

Multiple killers were inspired by *The Collector*.

In 1963, English author John Fowles published his debut novel *The Collector*, about a young male psychopath who kidnaps and imprisons a female student. Bob Bedrella, "the Kansas City Butcher," said in the confession of his serial murders that *The Collector* is what inspired him to kill. Charles Ng and Leonard Lake would later carry out a murder plot they called "Operation Miranda," named after the student in *The Collector*, Lake's favorite book.

Calvin Jones was acquitted because of a medical anomaly.

Philadelphia couple Calvin Jones and Sara Tolbert got into a fight one day in June 1964 inside a car, and it got so heated that Jones used a rubber hose to savagely beat Tolbert until she was unconscious. He drove around aimlessly with Tolbert in the car, but at some point in the next few hours she died. Jones turned himself in at a police station and admitted to murder. But then the medical examiner filed a surprising report: Tolbert had the blood disease sickle cell anemia, and she died from it while Jones was beating her. His murder charge turned into assault and battery.

A hit-and-run from 1968 was solved in 2012.

Four-year-old Carolee Sadie Ashby died in a hit-and-run auto accident in upstate New York in 1968. A drunk driver rolled through a stop sign at an intersection. Police investigated Douglas Parkhurst for the death, but he denied all knowledge of the crime and walked free. In 2012, retired Fulton City Police Department lieutenant Russ Johnson wrote about the cold case on a Facebook page about New York state history. A woman from the area who moved to Florida saw the post and wrote to police, telling them that years earlier, a relative of Parkhurst told her that they'd been in the car with the initial suspect, and that he had killed Ashby. The statute of limitations had expired, so Parkhurst was never convicted. But in 2018, in a bizarre twist of events, he was run over and killed on a baseball field by a woman having a psychotic episode.

A feared and presumed abduction was actually a multiple murder.

After sixteen-year-old David Brom didn't report to his Minnesota high school one day in February 1988, police at first believed that he'd been abducted. But then a rumor spread among students and staff that Brom had killed his parents and two of his three siblings. Administrators called police, and a friend of his clued them in: Brom had run off after skipping school that day to avoid capture. He'd killed his strict father with an ax, and then his mother, brother, and sister.

There are certain criteria for the "insanity defense."

Even though he was under eighteen, David Brom was tried as an adult because his crimes were so serious and committed in such a brutal fashion. His lawyer used an insanity defense, which brought attention to the legal use of the M'Naghten rule, a criterion developed in 1843 that determines whether a criminal was insane when committing a crime. It didn't work for Brom. Seven of the eight mental health professionals who evaluated Brom found him to be mentally competent. He received three life sentences for first-degree murder.

An entertainer killed an intruder and kept his body for decades.

Dorian Corey was an iconic player in New York's 1980s drag scene. When she died in 1993, her friends from the performance circuit went through her apartment and found a large garment bag buried deep in a closet. It smelled so bad that they called police, who discovered the long-dead, half-naked body of a man with a single bullet wound in his forehead. That solved the 1970s-era missing persons case of Bobby Worley, a felon convicted of rape and battery. Corey pinned a note to the body to explain why she shot Worley: "This poor man broke into my home and was trying to rob me."

Married killers worked both sides of the law.

Kirsten Davis was driving outside Vidalia, Georgia, around midnight on July 3, 1991, when a stranger pulled up beside her and fired a shotgun, sending a bullet into her head and causing her to lose control of the wheel. Later that night, married couple Tracy and Karen Wilkes came upon Davis's car, flipped over on the side of the road, and reported it to the police. Just forty-five days later, the Wilkeses burglarized and set ablaze the home of Moril Hudson after shooting Hudson in the head. The couple was later located in Alabama and charged with burglary, arson, and Hudson's murder, but due to a lack of evidence, they were never charged with Davis's murder.

A typo nearly sent a man to the execution chamber.

In 1987, Bruce Wayne Morris was found guilty of the first-degree murder of a hitchhiker he'd picked up near Sacramento. During sentencing, the judge informed the jury via a note that they had two choices: sentence Morris to death or life in prison with the possibility of parole. Except that the judge goofed; he'd meant to write *without* the possibility of parole. The jury, feeling their hand was forced, issued the death sentence. Morris's attorneys appealed, and fourteen years later, the sentence was vacated.

A killer killed again at his welcome-back-from-prison party.

Steven Pratt was just fifteen years old when he shot and killed his neighbor, Michael Anderson, in 1984. Tried as an adult, he received a thirty-year prison sentence for first-degree murder. He was released in 2014, and just two days later, following a "welcome home" party, Pratt beat his mother to death, sending him right back to prison.

Some cold cases intentionally become cold cases.

The town of Skidmore, Missouri, loathed Ken McElroy, and with good reason. After dodging charges for theft of livestock and property, burglary, arson, and assault, he attacked and impregnated a twelve-year-old, and to avoid prosecution, he strong-armed her parents into letting him marry her. In 1981, he beat a murder charge, but very quickly after his release, McElroy was repeatedly shot in public with sixty people watching. No paramedics were called, and nobody helped him. The murderer was never identified.

Kenneth Parks played the "sleepwalking" card.

In May 1987, Kenneth Parks drove fourteen miles across Toronto to the home of his wife's parents and attacked his in-laws, stabbing his mother-in-law to death and nearly bludgeoned his father-in-law to death. Just after the crimes, Parks drove to a police station and confessed. During the crime, Parks would later testify, he'd been asleep. He was later acquitted of the murder, with a court agreeing that the tremendous stress and health problems that caused his sleepwalking made him unaccountable for his actions.

CHAPTER 4

THE HUSBAND DID IT

It's a dark but well-known cliché
that when a woman in a relationship
featured in a true crime book dies,
her murderer is, almost without fail,
her spouse (or boyfriend).

John List left his family in sleeping bags and then dropped out of society.

John List was an exemplary member of the community, a prominent Westfield, New Jersey, banker and high-ranking member in his Lutheran church. Then in 1971, police got an anonymous tip (probably from List) to check out the List home. In the mansion's ballroom, they found the bodies of List's wife, his mother, and his three teenage children laid out on sleeping bags with their faces covered. They'd been dead for a month, by which time List had moved to Denver (and later, Virginia) and established a new identity as Robert Clark.

A realistic bust of John List got him caught.

In 1989, *America's Most Wanted* aired a segment about the unsolved List murders and hired a forensic sculptor to make a bust of what List would look like in the present day. Within a week, *AMW* got so many tips based on the extremely accurate bust that John List was arrested and confessed within a week.

Rene Castellani's wife-killing weapon of choice was tainted milkshakes.

Esther Castellani started to get ill in 1965, suffering stomach and back pain. Around that time, she also found a love letter addressed to her husband, popular Vancouver radio personality Rene Castellani. She confronted him, but nothing came of it. She got sicker, suffering nausea, diarrhea, vomiting spells, and paralysis. She died in August 1965 at age forty. An autopsy found 1,500 times the normal level of arsenic in her body; Rene had killed his wife so he could carry on with his radio station's receptionist. How he did it: milkshakes. Every day, Rene brought Esther a vanilla milkshake, and she never suspected he'd laced it with increasingly high amounts of arsenic.

An aristocrat killed the wrong woman by mistake.

Lord Lucan was a British playboy type who came from a moneyed, aristocratic family. In 1974, shortly after a bitter and acrimonious divorce from his wife, Veronica, in which she won custody of their children, Lucan sneaked into her London home and killed her. Or at least he thought he did. The room was dark, so he hadn't realized that the person he had bludgeoned to death with a lead pipe was his children's nanny, Sandra Rivett.

Lord Lucan's whereabouts are unknown but tricky.

Before he could be arrested or tried, Lord Lucan disappeared. According to popular theories, this is what happened to him: He drowned himself in Newhaven Harbor, he died by suicide with a gun handed to him by his friends (and had his remains fed to the lions at a private zoo in Kent), or he escaped to Australia and is living in a Buddhist retreat.

The disappearance of one woman led to her husband's conviction for a different murder.

Stacy Peterson disappeared from her home in Bolingbrook, Illinois, in 2007, and her body was never recovered. Suspicion fell on her husband, Drew Peterson, a former police officer who had been married three times previously, including to Kathleen Savio, who died under murkier circumstances. The nationwide media attention brought on by Stacy Peterson's death led police to open a file on Savio's death, and it uncovered enough evidence to send Peterson to prison for life. He eventually confessed to murdering both women.

Stacy Peterson and her mother both disappeared under suspicious circumstances.

Before her own disappearance and presumed untimely death, Stacy Peterson was no stranger to family tragedy. Nine years earlier, Christie Cales, Stacy's forty-year-old mother, suspiciously vanished. A known abuser of drugs and alcohol, she was living with a boyfriend in Illinois when on March 11, 1998, she walked out of her front door to meet a friend and simply vanished. Her case remains a mystery.

A wrestler's employer seemingly knew about his murders before authorities did.

Over a three-day period in 2007, WWE professional wrestler Chris Benoit strangled his wife, smothered his young son, and then killed himself. Fourteen hours before investigators believe the first murder occurred, an anonymous editor changed the wrestler's Wikipedia page to mention that Benoit had been fired from the WWE "due to personal issues stemming from the death of his wife Nancy." The IP address came from the city where WWE is headquartered.

One repeat murderer was caught because he killed his wives in similar ways.

Englishman George Smith got married in 1898, under the name George Love, and then from 1908 to 1914, he got married five more times, illegally and bigamously. He didn't have to juggle all those wives, however, because he killed them. He drowned Bessie Williams in her bathtub, persuading officials to write it up as an accidental death so he could inherit her estate. Five months later, he killed wife Alice Smith, making it look like an accident. But after he drowned Margaret Lloyd, Smith's old landlord read about the death, noticed George, and thought the death was eerily similar to the death of Alice Smith. In 1915, George Smith was executed for his crimes.

The sister of a victim tracked down a persistent Parisian wife-killer.

After splitting from his wife in 1914, when many women had lost husbands in World War I, Paris-born Henry Landru placed personal ads in French newspapers posing as a wealthy widower looking for a new bride. From 1915 to 1919, Landru attracted eleven lonely women to one of his two homes, robbed them of their money, murdered and dismembered them, and burned their bodies in his oven. He was finally caught when the sister of one of his victims tracked him down.

Philip Carl Jablonski wasn't rehabilitated, it would seem.

While initially a serial rapist, Philip Carl Jablonski wound up in prison, when he ventured to try murder. In 1978, he killed his ex-girlfriend (and the mother of his child), Linda Kimball. While in prison, Jablonski placed a newspaper ad looking for pen pals, and in 1982, Carol Spadoni responded. They fell in love over letters. Jablonski was paroled in 1990, and was believed to be rehabilitated. Instead, he went back to his old ways. He murdered four women, including Spadoni and her mother, Eva Peterson, soon after his release, and was sentenced to death for murder.

A German émigré married fifty women and killed many of them for money.

Johann Hoch was already married (for the second time) when he left his wife and children in what's now Germany to immigrate to the U.S. in 1887. He illegally married, committing bigamy, on the ship that took him to America. Over the next eighteen years, and with the help of twenty fake names, he married fifty different women. He moved constantly, attracting wealthy widows, whom he'd poison with arsenic, steal cash and jewelry from, and leave for dead. He was finally stopped in 1905 and convicted of just one murder—that of his last wife, Marie Walcker.

A serial poisoner went to prison for other reasons.

It's highly likely that Alfred Leonard Cline murdered as many as nine people between 1930 and 1945, including eight women he married so he could inherit their estates. They all died the same way: by drinking buttermilk laced with fatal doses of sedatives. For that he was dubbed "Buttermilk Bluebeard" by the media, but prosecutors couldn't make any of the murder charges stick. He ultimately received a 126-year prison sentence for nine counts of forgery.

A man married multiple women at once and then killed them.

James Watson was fairly reckless with Canadian and American bigamy laws in the late nineteenth and early twentieth centuries. To find women, he placed personal ads in various small-town newspapers. He managed to marry twenty-two different women, most of them simultaneously. There was even a period when he was married to three women who all lived within a few miles of one another. He wasn't caught until 1919, when he flat-out asked his newest wife, Kathryn Wombacher of Spokane, Washington, for a large amount of money. She hired a private detective, who broke into Watson's personal effects and uncovered multiple wedding rings and marriage licenses. He'd later admit to killing seven of his brides. He was sentenced to life in prison.

A murderer's father persuaded his son to confess.

In August 2018, Chris Watts's pregnant wife and their two daughters disappeared. Watts sat for media interviews where he seemed remarkably coolheaded and unfazed by the fact that his family was missing. His father quickly flew to Denver to provide comfort and support to his son, but just days later, he persuaded Chris Watts to turn himself in and confess to triple murder.

A man tried to kill his ex-girlfriend but died while lying in wait.

After Donna Miller broke off their relationship, Ricky Simonds went to her home in North Carolina in 1986 and strangled her to death. He was sentenced to twenty years in prison, but he was paroled in 1992. Sixteen years later, Simonds's girlfriend Kim Sprenger broke things off with him, and was so afraid of Simonds that she filed for a restraining order. When she drove home from work one day in June 2008, she noticed a horrible smell in her car. When she opened the trunk, she discovered Simonds's dead body. Police believe he planned to pop out and kill Sprenger, but that he died of heat exhaustion before he got the chance.

A Brazilian soccer star killed his mistress with the help of his wife.

Star Brazilian soccer goaltender Bruno Fernandes de Souza, known professionally as Bruno, met his mistress Eliza Samudio at a party. In 2009, when she got pregnant, Bruno urged her to terminate. She refused, and instead sued him for child support. He responded by kidnapping, torturing, and killing her. His accomplices included his cousin and his wife, to whom he'd been unfaithful.

A police officer killed his lover and love child to avoid supporting them.

Married Washington, D.C., police officer Richmond Phillips fathered a child with his mistress, Wynetta Wright. In June 2011, he shot and killed Wright, and then killed his nearly one-year-old baby by leaving her inside a hot car. His motive for the crimes that earned him two life sentences: He didn't want to get stuck making child support payments.

A former cop hired his son to kill his mistress.

Ex–Chicago police officer Devin Bickham Sr. got his mistress, Chevron Alexander, pregnant, but he knew he didn't want to marry her and raise their child, so he ordered a hit. He paid Devin Bickham Jr., his son, and another man to fatally shoot Alexander. The plot was carried out, but they were caught. The elder Bickham got ninety-five years in prison; the younger Bickham received fifty years.

A scorned ex-boyfriend killed an up-and-coming rock guitarist's mother and almost got away with it.

In 1983, Connie Navarro was murdered along with her friend, Sue Jory, at Jory's home. Her son, Dave Navarro, who would later play guitar for Jane's Addiction and the Red Hot Chili Peppers, was fifteen years old at the time, and had spent the night at his father's. Police failed to make any arrests in the double homicide until after the case was featured on a 1991 episode of *America's Most Wanted*. A viewer tip led police to chief suspect John Riccardi—the boyfriend that Connie Navarro had broken up with just before her death. He was captured and sentenced to life in prison without parole.

Tina Watson died suspiciously on her honeymoon.

Just eleven days after her wedding, Tina Watson died while on her honeymoon, an hour into a seven-day scuba diving trip in Australia. A pathologist determined that Watson died by drowning, but how that happened was unclear. Gabe Watson acted strangely after the murder, showing off a photo of his deceased wife near a sign that read "Caution: Drowning." According to Australian law enforcement, he offered sixteen stories about the circumstances that led to the death of his wife. Gabe Watson entered a guilty plea of manslaughter and served eighteen months in Australia. He had to stand trial again when he returned home to Alabama, this time for murder. The case, however, was dismissed.

A diplomat got away with murder and is still at large.

Career diplomat Brad Bishop Jr. worked for the U.S. State Department in Washington, D.C. One day in 1976, when he found out that he wouldn't be getting a promotion he expected, Bishop left work saying he felt ill and never returned. Eventually the Bishops' neighbors noticed that the whole family hadn't been home for a week. Police conducted a wellness check and found extensive property damage and blood spatter. Nobody was there. Police found the bodies of five of the six Bishops, everyone but Brad, far away in North Carolina. Brad Bishop's car turned up in the Great Smoky Mountains in Tennessee. As for Bishop himself, he was spotted three times in Europe, but he remains at large and wanted for the deaths of his family members.

Robert Fisher killed his wife and then disappeared into nature.

After Robert Fisher's wife told him that she wanted a divorce, he grew irate. On April 10, 2001, he shot his wife in the head, slashed the throats of their children, and set their Arizona home ablaze. Fisher's car was discovered, but Fisher himself never was. A trained survivalist who had purchased camping gear a few days before the murders, Robert Fisher is probably still living off the grid somewhere.

Scott Falater claimed to have killed his wife while sleepwalking.

Late one night in January 1997, Scott Falater of Phoenix used a hunting knife to stab his wife, Yarmila Falater, forty-four times. He then killed his dog in the same fashion, and tried to dispose of all the evidence. When Falater was eventually captured, he confessed to killing his wife, but he had a caveat: He said he was asleep while he committed the murder, so he shouldn't be held accountable. Prosecution poked holes in his sleepwalking defense by pointing out that the Falaters' marriage was troubled, and stating that Yarmila was considering leaving the marriage because he didn't want to have more children. Without a solid medical history of sleepwalking to pull from, that defense fell apart, and a court convicted Scott Falater of murder.

A lie detector snagged Adam Prout.

Wealthy British landowner Adam Prout killed his estranged wife, Kate Prout, in 2007 and buried her remains on his enormous estate in the English countryside. He steadfastly proclaimed his innocence through arrest and conviction, and his new fiancée did the same, until Prout confessed when he was told he'd be given a lie detector test.

The wife of a man with a secret family dies unexpectedly.

In 2003, socialite Jean Ann Cone drove home from a fundraiser with a friend tailing to make sure the seventy-five-year-old arrived there safely. Cone drove into the garage, closed the door, and was never seen alive again. Days later, Cone's daughter found her still in the driver's seat. Tests revealed that her blood alcohol level was double the state limit, and that she'd died of accidental car exhaust inhalation. Two weeks later, husband Douglas Cone remarried without telling his adult children. Police reopened the inquiry, and discovered that the new wife, Hillary Carlson, was already married to a man named Donald Carlson. Despite running in similar circles, the two men never appeared at the same functions at the same time—that's because they were the same person.

CHAPTER 5

LADY KILLERS

The vast majority of
criminals, particularly killers,
are men, so when a woman kills,
it's even more shocking.

Women in a Hungarian village in World War I poisoned their unwanted men.

During World War I, the town of Nagyrev, Hungary, became the site of a POW camp. With most of the men away fighting, the women were free to take up with many of the enemy soldiers. When the newly emboldened women's husbands returned from war, they could no longer live as they pleased. Those who were abused or bored by their husbands consulted Julia Fazekas, the town midwife. She offered them a solution in the form of arsenic she made by boiling flypaper and skimming poison off the top. Somewhere between fifty and three hundred men were killed indirectly by Fazekas before the Hungarian government stepped in and arrested twenty-six women, including her.

Wanda Holloway was killing to get her daughter onto the cheerleading squad.

Wanda Holloway was so desperate for her daughter, Shanna Harper, to make the cheerleading squad of her Houston high school in 1991 that she handed out pencils labeled with the kid's name. Doing so disqualified Shanna, so Holloway took more drastic measures—she murdered her neighbor, whose daughter, Amber, she theorized, would be too distraught to attend cheerleader tryouts. That would open up a spot for Shanna. When she asked her brother-in-law to find her a hitman, he went to the authorities, who outfitted him with a wire so he could gather evidence to prove Holloway's guilt when they next met. (Shanna never did make the team.)

Diane Downs killed her children because she thought that was what her boyfriend wanted.

In May 1983, Diane Downs was driving with her three children near Springfield, Oregon, when, during what Downs claimed was an attempted carjacking, a man shot and killed Downs's daughter and paralyzed her other two children. Forensic and blood spatter evidence proved Downs was lying; court testimony from the surviving daughter revealed that Downs pulled the trigger. She'd aimed to execute them so that she could carry on an affair with a married man who didn't like children.

Belle Gunness made a fortune killing and collecting insurance.

In 1902, Norwegian immigrant Belle Gunness married a butcher in Chicago. Just one week after they married, his baby daughter died while in Gunness's care. Unsurprisingly, she had taken out an insurance policy on the infant. Within the year, the butcher also died, but Gunness was found not guilty. He had died on the exact day that his two life insurance policies overlapped, so Gunness made a good profit. She then placed an ad for a new husband in midwestern newspapers, offering to "join fortunes." Gunness killed four men who came to her home responding to the ad. She stole their money and buried their bodies around the property, and somehow avoided capture. She ran off before police could find her, and despite having killed up to forty people in similar schemes, she was never found or prosecuted.

Serial killer Aileen Wuornos was captured after she crashed a victim's car.

Aileen Wuornos was found guilty of the deaths of six men in 1989 and 1990. All of those men were killed in self-defense, Wuornos argued, as they had tried to assault her when she was working as a prostitute. She went after a seventh male victim, but when she stole his car and got into an accident with it, police discovered that the vehicle was stolen and took Wuornos into custody.

An American woman served only a few hours for murder.

Laurie Ann Rogers was a victim of serial physical abuse by her husband, but what made her snap in 2004 was discovering that her husband had raped and impregnated her teenage daughter from a previous marriage and videotaped the act. She shot him while he slept, and tried to make it look like suicide. When her story didn't hold, she pled guilty to manslaughter. Judge Paul A. Hackner sympathized. He suspended the sentence, giving credit for time served, and released her that day.

The only two women to receive life sentences in the U.K. hated each other.

In 2014, spree killer Joanna Dennehy was admitted to the same prison in Middlesex, England, that housed child killer Rosemary West. Within five to twenty minutes of her arrival there, Dennehy threatened to kill West. She was determined to be top dog in the hierarchy, and West was her only competition. West was placed in solitary confinement, and then transferred a day later for her safety.

A British killer just wanted to see what it felt like to kill.

Joanna Dennehy was a spree killer, ending the lives of five men in just a ten-day period in England in 2013. She stabbed all of her victims: three of whom she knew personally, and the other two she chose randomly. Why'd she do it? She explained it to her psychiatrist in the best way she could: "I killed to see how I would feel, to see if I was as cold as I thought I was. Then it got more-ish."

A former professional wrestler killed old ladies with medical equipment.

Juana Barraza was a former wrestler who found more fame (or infamy) as a killer. Posing as a government nurse, she'd help elderly women carry their groceries inside, or she'd offer to clean their kitchen, and then she'd bludgeon or strangle them to death with a stethoscope or phone cable. Barraza was officially charged with eleven murders between 1998 and 2006, but she may have killed as many as forty-nine people.

Sharon Kinnie tried to pawn off the murder of her husband on her toddler daughter.

In 1960, Sharon Kinnie's husband was fatally shot in the head. Kinnie told investigators that their two-year-old daughter had been playing with a gun and had accidentally shot her father. They bought it at the time, but when she later killed the wife of one of her lovers, it was clear that she had lied. Kinnie evaded capture, and she is still on the run. She now has the longest outstanding arrest warrant for murder in the history of Kansas City, Missouri, and one of the longest outstanding felony warrants in U.S. history.

Lavinia Fisher ran an inn-meets-murder-house with her husband.

Lavinia Fisher is America's first female serial killer. She was hanged, along with her husband John Fisher, for highway robbery in 1820. They had started their life of crime as owners of an inn just outside of Charleston, South Carolina, where they would invite wealthy men to dinner, drop them into the basement via a bedroom trapdoor, and then kill them with an ax.

A man who escaped a murder house was later robbed by his would-be killers.

John Peoples escaped John and Lavinia Fisher's infamous death trap–laden boardinghouse in the early nineteenth century, only to be robbed by a group of highway robbers who stole $40 from him. Among that band of robbers were John and Lavinia Fisher.

Nannie Doss enjoyed poisoning her relatives.

In October 1954, Samuel Doss checked into a Tulsa hospital complaining of severe gastrointestinal discomfort. He died, and the autopsy revealed high amounts of arsenic in his vital organs. That's when his wife, Nannie, admitted to poisoning him to death, just like she'd done with three other husbands, two of her children, her grandson, and her mother.

Two lovers-then-murderers blamed each other, and both met their end.

In 1927, Ruth Brown Snyder and her lover, Henry Judd Gray, were put on trial for the murder of Snyder's husband, Albert Snyder. They unsuccessfully made the death look like a burglary gone wrong because Snyder wanted to collect the $100,000 life insurance policy she had taken out on her husband. After they were caught, she blamed Gray, and Gray blamed her. Both of them claimed that the other one was the ringleader who forced them to go along with the plan. In the end, they were both executed in the electric chair.

A poisoned chocolate delivery led to murder charges.

In August 1898, Mary Dunning received a delivery of chocolates to her home in Delaware with a note attached that read, "With love to yourself and baby. —Mrs. C." Dunning and some friends ate up, and within days, Dunning and one of the friends were dead from arsenic poisoning. "Mrs. C" ended up being Cordelia Botkin, the mistress of John Dunning. He had broken it off just before she sent the poisoned chocolates all the way from California.

A convicted murderer lived it up and got romanced in a women's prison.

Cordelia Botkin was tried and convicted in California for killing her lover's wife and a friend with arsenic-laced chocolates, and was sentenced to life in prison. She immediately filed an appeal and was imprisoned in San Quentin in the interim, and during that time started two affairs with two guards, who brought her special banned items and even took her out on dates. By 1910, however, she was dead. Her affairs alone could not sustain her. The death certificate listed the cause of death as "softening of the brain, due to melancholy."

Blond women don't go to jail as often as brunettes do.

According to courtroom and jury trial experts, women prosecuted for serious crimes are much less likely to be convicted if they've got blond hair. However, if they're on trial for crimes of criminal negligence, blonds are *more* likely to be found guilty.

A retail employee was murdered over leggings.

Two women at a Lululemon Athletica store in Bethesda, Maryland, were seemingly attacked by a masked robber in March 2011. Employee Jayna Murray died, while another employee named Brittany Norwood survived. Police soon uncovered the truth: There was no group of masked male robbers. Norwood confessed to trying to steal leggings. When Murray confronted her, Norwood had unleashed hell, bludgeoning and stabbing Murray to death. Then she gave herself some wounds, bound her own hands and feet, and lay next to the dead body to divert suspicion.

A blogger blogged about her son's death, which she caused.

Lacey Spears started a blog from her Chestnut Ridge, New York, home, detailing her thoughts and feelings about her son who was dying of a mysterious illness. Her blog garnered hits and sympathy alike. The truth, though, was that she had Munchausen syndrome by proxy and was inducing illness in her child to gain attention. Her son died of slow salt poisoning.

A teenager hired a killer to murder her parents, and her father figured it out.

Wealthy auto parts executive Huei Hann Pan and his wife, Bich Ha Pan, were the victims of a home invasion, and were robbed at gunpoint by Lenford Crawford and David Mylvaganam in 2010. Bich died of three gunshot wounds to the head, while Huei recovered with bullet fragments in his face, a broken bone near his eye, and a broken neck bone. He fell into a coma, but strangely his daughter, Jennifer Pan, wasn't hurt at all: She was left tied to a banister and she later was able to get away and call the police. She told the police that she heard an argument and gunshots. When her father awoke, he remembered everything: Jennifer had conversed with the robbers "like a friend" before the violence began. She'd hired the duo for $2,500 to kill her parents.

Statistical improbability is what got Marybeth Tinning arrested.

In the 1970s, all nine children under the care of Marybeth Tinning—eight biological and one adopted—died of natural causes. At least, that's what she said and what doctors initially believed, citing various causes of death, including genetic conditions, meningitis, seizures, cardiac arrest, and pneumonia. It wasn't until after the death of her ninth child, four-month-old Tami Lynne, that police started to get suspicious. In 1986, Tinning admitted to smothering three of her children, and was convicted in the death of Tami Lynne.

Only a small percentage of murders in the U.S. are committed by women.

Only 15 percent of serial killers are women, and only 10 percent of single-act murderers are women. That works out to about 11 percent of all premeditated killings in the United States. Women also overwhelmingly choose poison as their weapon of choice, and are far more likely to be victims of murder than perpetrators: 65 percent of serial killers' victims are women.

A nineteenth-century English woman collected babies to collect checks.

In the 1890s in England, Amelia Dyer set up what's known as a "baby farming" operation. Just as some people abuse the foster care system by taking in as many children as possible to collect multiple checks from the state to pay for their care, Dyer received a flat fee from the government to take in abandoned and orphaned infant children. Then she killed them with liquid opiates or slowly starved them to death, depending on how quickly she wanted to be rid of them.

SIDS didn't kill Waneta Hoyt's children— she did.

Between 1965 and 1971, all five of Waneta Hoyt's children died from "crib death," or sudden infant death syndrome, a still-baffling condition wherein a baby suddenly dies with little or no symptoms or warning. In the 1960s, SIDS was considered a public health crisis, and medical journals wrote about Hoyt's situation hoping to find some kind of genetic cause for SIDS. Other medical writers found the instance of five children all dying of SIDS to be mathematically and statistically impossible. It wasn't until the 1990s that Hoyt confessed to killing all five of her children. She later recanted that confession, but only after she'd been sentenced to seventy-five years in prison.

A British "baby farmer" returned to killing infants after her prison term.

In 1879, after a number of babies died in her care, Amelia Dyer was sentenced to six months of hard labor for the crime of neglect. She resumed her baby farming operations after her sentence was over, and she became more violent and careless, strangling infants and then abandoning them in rivers. A body was traced back to her; she confessed, and was sentenced to death in 1896. It's unknown how many children she killed, but it was likely in the hundreds.

Tillie Klimek's psychic abilities were a big clue as to who she'd kill next.

In the 1920s and 1930s, Tillie Klimek married three times in the Chicago area, finding a new husband after each one died. Klimek mystified and frightened family and friends with her so-called psychic abilities: Before each of her three husbands' deaths, she claimed to have had dreams in which she learned the exact dates of their passing. In reality, Klimek was putting rat poison in her husbands' food, and her "prediction" was actually just her announcement of when she planned to murder them.

An old nursery rhyme is based on a real murder case.

Canadian schoolchildren in the 1940s and 1950s sang a popular playground song that was similar to "Ring Around the Rosie." It went like this: "You cut off his legs, you cut off his arms, you cut off his head, how could you, Mrs. Dick?" That schoolyard song actually refers to the 1946 death of Russian immigrant John Dick, presumably at the hands of his new wife, Evelyn MacLean Dick. She was acquitted of murder, but found guilty of manslaughter for another death, and her father was found guilty of being an accessory to the murder of John Dick.

"The Merry Widow of Windy Nook" killed before the wedding food could spoil.

In the 1950s, residents of the community of Windy Nook, England, clearly thought something was up with Mary Elizabeth Wilson. She had earned the nickname "the Merry Widow of Windy Nook." In a five-year period, she had married four men who had all died shortly after the wedding, some within a matter of weeks. She was married to each of them long enough to establish herself as the chief heir to their substantial estates. She was aware of her reputation, too. When asked by a friend what to do with leftovers from a wedding reception, she quipped, "We'll keep them for the funeral." In 1958, the bodies of her husbands were exhumed, and all contained substantial amounts of insecticide. She was sentenced to life in prison, but she died just four years later at age seventy.

Mrs. Dick was curiously paroled and pardoned after committing two familial murders.

John Dick's body—reduced to a limbless, headless torso—was found by five children in a forest in Hamilton, Ontario. Once the body was identified, police searched the home of Dick's estranged wife, Evelyn Dick. They found his partially burned limbs in the furnace and a suitcase containing concrete and the body of her baby son. She served eleven years in prison, was paroled in 1958, and posthumously pardoned in 1985 for reasons not revealed to the public.

Police found an extra victim when investigating the disappearance of Don Beets.

Betty Lou Beets filed a missing persons report in August 1983 for Don Beets, her fifth husband. His unmanned boat was found in a lake, and his death was attributed to an accidental drowning. But two years later, Beets's son confessed to police that he'd helped his mother bury Don Beets's corpse. His remains were found hidden under a garden ornament along with another body they weren't even looking for, that of Doyle Wayne Baker, Beets's deceased fourth husband. Both had been shot in the back of the head.

A boardinghouse proprietor openly used rat poison to kill (and then rob) her charges.

Amy Archer-Gilligan ran a boardinghouse for the elderly and infirm in the 1910s in Windsor, Connecticut. Between 1911 and 1916, forty-eight people died in Archer-Gilligan's nursing home, all of them just after making a hefty $1,000 long-term care payment or changing their wills to name their caretaker as the beneficiary of their life insurance policy. Acting on a tip from a suspicious sister of a deceased resident, a reporter for the *Hartford Courant* uncovered "the murder factory." Police got involved, and every exhumed body tested positive for poison (strychnine or arsenic). Local shopkeepers said Archer-Gilligan had frequently purchased large amounts of the stuff, which she said she used to kill rats.

Two teens enjoyed a movie date where they had just committed murder.

Police discovered forty-nine-year-old Elizabeth Edwards and her thirteen-year-old daughter, Katie Edwards, dead inside their home in Nottingham, England, in April 2016. Police quickly discovered the identity of their murderers: Elizabeth's other daughter, fourteen-year-old Kim Edwards, and her boyfriend, Lucas Markham. Immediately after stabbing the two women in the throat, the couple stayed in the house, took a bath, and watched a *Twilight* movie.

A teacher persuaded a student to kill her husband, and he figured it out with his last breath.

Wisconsin high school teacher's aide Diane Borchardt became so enraged when she learned that her husband, Ruben, had been carrying on an extramarital affair that she persuaded a student at Jefferson High School to kill the man. Douglas Vest agreed to commit the crime for a $20,000 fee after she fed him false stories of abuse at the hands of her husband. He recruited two friends to help him out. The teens broke into the Borchardt home and killed him. Ruben's dying words to his son were, "I can't believe she would do this to me." A friend of the three high schoolers tipped off police and all parties were arrested.

An Australian woman had her father killed while she eavesdropped.

Nicknamed Belinda "Van Evil" by the Australian press, Belinda Van Krevel asked her boyfriend to kill her father with an ax while he slept. As Keith Schreiber committed the bloody murder in 2000, Belinda and her two-year-old daughter listened through a wall. Later, when she was pinpointed as the mastermind behind the murder, Van Krevel admitted that she'd wanted her father dead because he'd allegedly assaulted her daughter. After six years in prison, Van Krevel was released, but she was soon arrested for the brutal stabbing of her new boyfriend.

Everyone in a love triangle had a hand in the death of Julian Lewis.

While in romantic relationships with both Matthew Shallenberger and Rodney Fuller, Teresa Lewis asked the men to work together to kill her husband, Julian Lewis, and her stepson, Charles Lewis. Lewis provided the guns and ammunition for the crime and left her door unlocked so the men could sneak in at night and kill their targets as they slept. She watched as they were murdered, then waited forty-five minutes to call police. When they arrived, Julian Lewis was still alive and delivered his last words: "My wife knows who done this to me." He died soon after.

A Utah man was shot for assaulting a woman telepathically.

In 2011, Meloney Selleneit asked her husband to tell Utah police that their neighbor Tony Pierce was sexually assaulting her—with his brain, harnessing the power of telepathy. Police didn't respond to the situation, so the Selleneits took the law into their own hands. Michael Selleneit shot Pierce at the request of his wife when Pierce was standing on a ladder outside his home. Surprisingly, Pierce survived, and shockingly, the Selleneits passed a mental competency exam and were found psychologically fit to stand trial for attempted murder.

A phony CIA agent led to deadly retaliation against so-called bullies.

In 2012, Marvin Potter and Jamie Curd, Jenelle Potter's father and boyfriend, broke into the home of Tennessee couple Billy Payne and Billie-Jean Hayworth and shot them. They were the hired hands; the murder was orchestrated by Jenelle Potter and her mother. Her motive: She felt left out when her crush, Payne, and Hayworth started dating. She told her parents that the couple had bullied her online, then created a phony CIA agent profile to convince her mother that the bullying was real. Jenelle and her mother, Barbara Potter, got the two men to do the job, which occurred in front of the victims' infant son.

In his suicide note, a police officer confessed to murdering his mistress's spouse.

Bruce Miller was sitting in his Michigan office in 1999 when somebody walked in and shot him. Police had no leads. They chalked up the death to a robbery gone wrong. The cold case got hot again a year later when former police officer Jerry Cassaday committed suicide. In his suicide note, he confessed to killing Miller with the help of his lover, Sharee Miller, the victim's wife. After sixteen years of professing her innocence behind bars, Sharee Miller finally confessed.

A mother used her teenage daughter to commit a crime.

Anthony and Anne Marie Anastasi had an open relationship, sometimes entertaining Jacqueline Riggs as their third party in the bedroom. After they moved in together in 2015, Anne Marie reported her husband and Riggs dead in what she said was a murder-suicide. Police didn't believe her, however, after a ballistics test proved that the gun at the crime scene didn't match the caliber of the bullets found in both victims. In the end, Anastasi's thirteen-year-old daughter admitted to the double murder. She said she was acting on her mother's behalf.

An ice cream shop proprietor had bodies frozen in the basement.

Estibaliz Carranza owned an ice cream parlor in Vienna, Austria, in the early 2000s, but she most aspired to be a mother. When the two men to whom she was romantically attached failed to get her pregnant, Carranza murdered them and stored the bodies in the basement of her popular ice cream shop, with their dismembered parts placed in freezers, tubs, and concrete blocks, and their smell covered up by air fresheners. Her ice cream–making machinery reportedly made a cover for the noise she made with her body-cutting chainsaw.

Two women ran a cult and both scammed and killed their followers.

In 1922, mother-daughter con artists May Blackburn and Ruth Rizzio created a quasi-religious movement called the Divine Order of the Royal Arms of the Great Eleven, claiming that archangels had revealed to them the sites of valuable treasures. They built a commune for their large following in Simi Valley, California, and while their crimes consisted of stealing their adherents' money and committing grand theft, they also performed ritual animal sacrifices. They built a brick oven, into which they placed Florence Turner. They assured her that its holy fires would cure her blood disease. Instead, she was baked alive.

A member of the Manson family tried to kill the president.

Lynette Fromme, known widely as Squeaky due to the high-pitched timbre of her voice, joined Charles Manson's cult at age nineteen after dropping out of college and feeling depressed. She wasn't involved in the Tate-LaBianca murders, but she was charged with contempt of court and attempting to prevent other followers from testifying, subsequently serving short prison sentences. In 1975, long after the Manson cult had dissolved due to the incarceration of most of its members, Fromme attempted to assassinate President Gerald Ford, though she claimed that her gun accidentally fired when she was just trying to talk to the politician about environmental issues.

A jealous lover orchestrated a skydiving death.

Els Clottermans and Els Van Doren shared first names as well as a boyfriend: Marcel Somers, whom they both met at their parachuting and skydiving club in Zwartberg, Belgium. Although Van Doren was married, the trio set up a sexual arrangement: Clottermans had access to Somers on Friday nights, and Van Doren on Saturdays. One Saturday night in 2006, Clottermans slept on Somers's couch and overheard Van Doren and Somers having relations. She became so jealous and resentful that she took Van Doren's parachute and sabotaged its release cord. A week later, the trio all went skydiving together, and, just as Clottermans had planned, Van Doren's parachute didn't work. She plummeted to her death. Clottermans was convicted of murder.

A woman was jealous of a happy couple, so she killed them.

Melanie Smith was called "the most evil woman in Britain" *by her own children* for the callous murder of five people in 2013. She lived in the downstairs flat of an apartment building, just below the couple Lee Anna Shiers and Liam Timbrell. They were by all accounts a gloriously happy couple. Smith was deeply unhappy in her relationship and often fought with her boyfriend, whom she suspected of infidelity. One day, she took out her displeasure on Shiers and Timbrell. After overhearing them having sex, Smith went upstairs and lit a baby carriage in the hallway on fire. The apartment burned, killing the couple, Timbrell's son, and Shiers's niece and nephew.

CHAPTER 6

Still Unsolved

Unfortunately, and tragically,
some of the most haunting and horrific
murders on Earth are never solved.

The Lover's Lane killer murdered couples regularly—until he or she just stopped.

Over ten weekends from February to May 1946, a killer stalked couples who'd parked in Lover's Lane areas in Texarkana, a Texas-Arkansas border town. The first couple attacked, Jimmy Hollis and Mary Jeanne Larey, survived. Then the killer murdered three more couples (one woman survived, but was seriously wounded). Texas Rangers patrolled the town for three months but left after the murders stopped. The Phantom Killer, as he or she was nicknamed, was never identified.

Chuck Morgan was found with a $2 bill and his own hanky-wrapped tooth.

Chuck Morgan was a financial manager in Tucson, Arizona. He was a potential witness in a fraud case with ties to the Mob. After disappearing for three days in March 1977, he returned, letting his wife know that his throat had been painted with a hallucinogenic drug that would kill him if he spoke. He recovered at home under her care, then disappeared two months later. Despite a call from a strange woman saying her husband was all right, Morgan's body was found in the desert forty miles outside of Tucson. He'd been shot in the back of the head with his own gun. His car was full of weapons, ammo, and one of Morgan's teeth wrapped in a hanky. He had a $2 bill strapped to his underwear with names on it. A woman named "Green Eyes" called the Pima County Sheriff saying Morgan had tried to pay off the assassin hired to kill him, and failed. But this was never proven and the case went cold.

Four decades later, authorities remain baffled by the oldest cold case in Delaware.

In 1977, a person walking along Old Union Church Road in Townsend, Delaware, spotted a body in a roadside drainage ditch. Police determined from the decomposed remains that the victim had been a woman in her forties, somewhere between five feet three and five feet six, and that she was murdered somewhere else. Despite using photographic technology to create reasonably accurate photos of what the deceased would have looked like while alive, Townsend police have never received a decent lead on her identity—and, thus, have no idea who killed her or why.

Edwin Matlock disappeared from his cabin forever.

In 1951, U.S. Armed Forces veteran Edwin Matlock was living on the outskirts of Spokane, Washington. His family spoke to him around March 1, but when he didn't show up for Thanksgiving dinner nearly nine months later, his mother went to his cabin, found him gone, and reported him missing. He apparently vanished, leaving behind only rumors about his whereabouts. Some said he moved to Alaska, or that he'd been shot, killed, and secretly buried by the husband of a married woman he'd been seeing. All of those leads turned up nothing, and no trace of Matlock was ever found.

DNA evidence proved unhelpful in solving the case of a young woman's stabbing.

The body of twenty-year-old Sandra Williams was found in a suburban neighborhood of Mobile, Alabama, on September 11, 1980. Authorities ruled that the woman had been stabbed to death. Williams's remains were discovered eight miles from her home, which had no signs of forced entry and where her car remained parked. No progress was made on the case until 2019, when newly discovered DNA evidence linked Alvin Ray Allen, arrested by Mobile police for an unrelated murder charge after a standoff with a SWAT team, to the crime. A jury wasn't convinced of his guilt in Williams's death, a mistrial was declared, and the case went cold again.

Debbie Spickler vanished on her way to a Connecticut swimming pool.

One evening in July 1968, thirteen-year-old Debbie Spickler decided to walk with her cousin to the swimming pool at Henry Park in Vernon, Connecticut. At some point on their walk, the cousin ran back home to get towels and Spickler continued heading to the pool. When the cousin arrived, she couldn't find Spickler anywhere because she never made it to the pool. She disappeared, and no trace of life or remains matching hers have been found. There's still a $50,000 reward for information.

Two Alaskan photographers found what they thought was a mutilated mannequin.

On Christmas Day 1971, brothers Dennis and Gary Lawler headed to McHugh Creek State Park in Alaska to take nature photos. Dennis peered over a ledge near a waterfall and saw what he thought was a mannequin, but it was a half-naked corpse, with hands tied with electrical wire and cuts on the chest. The murder victim was eighteen-year-old Beth van Zanten, who'd disappeared two days earlier from an Anchorage convenience store. Forensic investigation determined that van Zanten had been kidnapped and taken to McHugh Creek, where she was assaulted. She managed to escape, only to fall off a ledge and freeze to death where she landed. Police never fingered a culprit, not even Alaska-based serial killer Robert Hansen, who was active in the area in the early 1970s.

Authorities couldn't even figure out how the Jeatrans died, let alone who was responsible.

A friend of Nick and Jane Jeatran made a grisly discovery at their home in Clearwater, Florida, on Christmas Eve 1968. Through a window, she saw the elderly couple lying on the floor in their pajamas, covered in blood. Jane was already dead; Nick died of his injuries three days later. The going theory by Clearwater police was that the couple had woken up to a burglary in process and suffered violent deaths. They were both hit in the head with a blunt object, but detectives never determined what that murder weapon was, nor did they locate a solid suspect, or find the jewelry that the burglar stole.

A Prussian immigrant was shot by an unknown party during the California Gold Rush.

Herman Ehrenberg departed his homeland of Prussia to make it in America. He fought in the Texas Revolution, and then made a fortune as a miner and surveyor during the California Gold Rush. On the evening of October 9, 1866, while traveling by stagecoach from Yuma, Arizona, to San Bernardino, California, he slept overnight on a bench outside the stagecoach station in Dos Palmas. Stationmaster W. H. Smith, who slept inside, reported hearing a gunshot around midnight. He went out to find Ehrenberg shot, and dying from his wound, and he discovered that the general store had also been robbed. Two theories: A man from the Cahuilla Tribe robbed and killed Ehrenberg, or Smith killed him. There was never enough evidence to link either party, and the case is now the coldest case in California.

A missing judge somehow sneaked an envelope of money into his apartment.

Five months after his disappearance, Mrs. Joseph Carter finally returned to their apartment and found an envelope with $7,000 in cash and the judge's will, composed in 1925, along with a list of everyone to whom Carter owed money. He signed the letter, "Am very weary. Love, Joe." Detectives hadn't found the envelope in their many searches, and the twenty-four-hour watch hadn't seen anybody enter or leave the residence.

A New York judge disappeared, uncovering his criminal underworld connections.

In August 1930, just after his appointment to the New York Supreme Court, Judge Joseph Carter took a vacation in Maine with his wife, only to be called back to New York City. He told his wife that he had to "straighten those fellows out." Nine days later, he hadn't come back home, and his wife filed a missing persons report. He was never found, but investigators discovered that he'd been leading a double life, one that involved mistresses, political payoffs, fraud, bribery, and organized crime connections.

A police officer may have been the perpetrator in an unsolved Hawaii murder.

In January 1982 in Oahu, Hawaii, nineteen-year-old hairdresser Lisa Au left work and went to visit her boyfriend at his sister's apartment. She never made it back home. Her boyfriend found Au's car parked on a highway shoulder. Her window was partially rolled down, and her purse remained in the car with only her driver's license missing. Investigators believe a police officer (or someone posing as such) may have been involved in the disappearance—stopping Au, asking for her license, and then abducting her. A massive ten-day search of the entirety of Oahu commenced and ended when Au's body was found in a ravine. Her death remains unsolved.

An Idaho widow wasn't buried where police thought she'd be.

Fifty-one-year-old Lillian Richey returned to her home in Nampa, Idaho, late one night in 1964 after visiting a nightclub with an out-of-town male friend. The friend drove Richey's car back to his hotel, and returned it in the morning to take Richey out to breakfast, but she was gone. She didn't show up for work the next day either. When police investigated her disappearance, they found no signs of forced entry or struggle. The friend was cleared of wrongdoing. More than fifty years later, Nampa police acted on a theory that Richey was murdered and her remains tossed into the under-construction foundation of a school district administration building. A Boise State University archaeology class excavated there, but didn't find Richey's remains.

Jimmy Hoffa's body isn't where a mobster says he left it.

A powerful labor union leader with criminal underworld connections, Jimmy Hoffa flat-out disappeared after a dinner in Detroit in 1975. He was declared dead that same year, although federal agencies continue to search for his remains. In 1989, mobster Donald "Tony the Greek" Frankos claimed that he'd helped murder Hoffa, sent his remains to New Jersey in an oil drum, and had him buried in an end zone at Giants Stadium. The feds were skeptical, but when Giants Stadium was torn down in 2010, there was no trace of Hoffa.

For more than forty years, police in West Virginia haven't been able to determine who killed Annita Price.

Annita Price left home just before 9 P.M. on May 30, 1974, for her shift at the Flamingo Club in Benwood. She never arrived. The next day, her car was found a few towns away. Inside it were her purse, wallet, and makeup. There were no signs of a struggle. She was in the middle of a heated custody battle with her estranged husband, but he was cleared of any connection to the disappearance. In 2002, police acted on a tip and excavated part of a state highway where the body had allegedly been dumped. In 2016, cadaver dogs searched a nearby gypsum plant. Both searches turned up nothing.

Mary Virginia Carpenter's remains might have been found in a box ten years after her disappearance.

In June 1948, twenty-one-year-old Mary Virginia Carpenter arrived in Denton, Texas, to study at the Texas State College for Women. A cabdriver took her from the train station and dropped her off at her dormitory, and that's the last anyone saw of Carpenter. Ten years later, in Jefferson, Texas, authorities discovered a box containing the skull and skeletal remains of a woman whose description matched that of Carpenter, in that one leg was shorter than the other. But the dental records didn't match. Police never found Carpenter's remains, and they still don't know who this skeleton belongs to.

Jodi Serrin's parents walked in on her murder, but thought she was having sex.

Jodi Serrin suffered from mental illness but lived on her own in San Diego, with her parents checking in on her daily as a precautionary measure. On Valentine's Day 2007, they went to Serrin's residence, opened the bedroom door, and found their daughter in the middle of a vigorous physical encounter with a man. Embarrassed, they backed out, closed the door, and waited for Serrin to emerge. After waiting awhile, they went back in and found Serrin alone, dead and murdered, her body already gone cold. The man who was with her left out the window and was never identified.

Jessica Chambers's mouth was so badly burned that paramedics couldn't understand her when she identified her assailant.

Paramedics in Courtland, Mississippi, discovered Jessica Chambers next to her car, aflame, in December 2014. She was horribly burned over her entire body (except the bottoms of her feet). Gasoline had been poured on her body, down her throat, and up her nose, before she'd been set on fire. She was coherent enough to try to tell authorities who'd done this to her, but she'd been so mutilated by fire that they couldn't understand what she'd said. She died of her injuries the following morning. Paramedics who discovered Chambers later required counseling to deal with what they'd seen; police had a suspect in the case, but never issued any charges.

Dozens of confessions and odd clues didn't help police discover who killed the Black Dahlia.

The nude, halved, and bafflingly bloodless body of the Black Dahlia—aspiring actress Elizabeth Short—was found in a field in Los Angeles in January 1947. Short wore her hair black and favored black clothes, thus the nickname. Police were baffled by the details of her murder. They received a package with Short's ID, birth certificate, address book, and photographs of the actress with many men, all washed with gasoline to remove fingerprints. More than fifty men confessed to the murder, but none were found liable. The Black Dahlia murder remains unsolved.

There's compelling evidence that a Hollywood legend may have killed the Black Dahlia.

One possible suspect in the highly publicized, Hollywood-centered Black Dahlia murder case was big-time film actor Orson Welles. Around the time of the murder of Elizabeth Short, Welles was rumored to have made large payments to make rape charges go away. Some authorities believed that his quirky personality and fits of anger made him a likely culprit in Short's murder.

A nine-year-old girl left home and was spotted on a rural road in the middle of the night before she disappeared.

When Asha Degree's father checked on her at about 2:30 A.M. on February 14, 2000, she was asleep in her bed in their home in Cleveland County, North Carolina. When her mother went to wake her up at 6:30 A.M., she was gone. Witnesses would later say they spotted nine-year-old Asha walking along a rural highway, alone, in the rain. She was never heard from again—although her backpack was found miles away, inside of a trash bag, a year later. It's unclear what happened to Asha, or why she left home in the middle of the night.

Tim Molnar left home and wound up in a block of ice hundreds of miles away.

One morning in January 1984, nineteen-year-old Tim Molnar left home for a class at Embry-Riddle Aeronautical University in Daytona Beach, but never arrived. Four months later, his family received a letter from an impound lot in Atlanta—four hundred miles away—saying his car had been left there the week he'd vanished. His wallet with identification and credit card was left in the car. In 1996, Molnar's case was dramatized on NBC's *Unsolved Mysteries*, and a man called in a tip, saying he recognized Molnar's clothes from a body he found in a frozen block of ice in Wisconsin in 1986. DNA testing confirmed the body was Molnar.

A scream and a shadow were the only shreds of evidence in a murder case.

Portland, Indiana, teacher Garnet Ginn didn't show up at school one day in February 1950, so a worried district administrator and neighbor headed to the garage where Ginn stored her sports car. The garage happened to be on the same block as a police station. Ginn's body was there, hanging from a sewing machine belt attached to a door handle. The death was ruled a suicide, but Ginn's family had the body exhumed for an autopsy and found evidence of blunt force trauma and strangulation. A neighbor had reported a scream and said she saw a shadow in the garage on the night of Ginn's death, but that's all the evidence that ever emerged.

An enemy of the Nazis and the food industry wound up dead.

Louis B. Allyn changed the way Americans think about food thanks to his early 1900s exposé, *The Westfield Pure Food Book*, about recklessly processed food. The book led to the establishment of the FDA. This made him an enemy of the food production industry, and when he refused to turn over a valuable patent to the Nazis in the early 1940s, he was an enemy of the Nazis as well. Allyn was shot to death in his home in Massachusetts in 1940 while reading a book called *The Gun*. A lot of people wanted Allyn dead, but police could never figure out who killed him.

A beeper was the sole piece of evidence in the disappearance of an Arizona woman.

The body of Denise Johnson was found in a remote spot in Arizona in 1992, and investigators were stymied by an almost total lack of evidence. They were unable to recover any hair, saliva, or blood from the crime scene to lead them to the murderer. Near the crime scene, police found a beeper and traced it to truck driver Mark Bogan, who admitted to picking up Johnson while she was hitchhiking. He also admitted that they had sex in his truck. Then, he said, she robbed him and ran off with his beeper. The case remains unsolved.

A teenager left home to run errands and ended up dead in a Mississippi ravine.

One of the oldest cold cases in the United States concerns the July 1910 murder of eighteen-year-old Janie Sharp from the rural farming community of Rural Hill, Mississippi. After walking a mile into town for errands, she failed to return home. A search party formed at dusk, and her brother Lee followed a ravine, where he found the body of his sister, her throat slashed. The town suspected Swinton Parmenter, a local teen with a crush on Sharp, who was seen swimming near where Sharp was last seen alive. During the search, he told the others not to look in the ravine because he'd already checked it out. He was charged with murder and sentenced to death, but his conviction was reversed on appeal.

Police in New Mexico decided not to pursue an investigation into the death of a town villain.

The bloated, maggot-eaten, decapitated corpse of seventy-year-old Arthur Rochford Manby was found in his Taos, New Mexico, mansion by a federal marshal in 1929. Manby was easily the town's villain, on account of how he cheated numerous people out of their land and their mineral rights due to shady deals and connections with politicians. He was the subject of dozens of lawsuits at the time of his death. Local law enforcement didn't actively pursue the case.

The identity of a strangely dressed body with his pockets full of cash remains a mystery fifty years later.

While sledding in West Saugerties, New York, in February 1970, two kids spotted a corpse at the end of an embankment. The identity of neither the victim nor his assailant has ever been determined. The man had been shot in the back of the head, gang-execution style. He was also dressed strangely, with a raincoat on top of a suit, on top of pajamas, and he had $156 in his pockets.

The property belonging to a small-town kook was discovered to house many mysteriously murdered bodies.

Eugene Butler was a polarizing figure in tiny Niagara, North Dakota, in the early 1900s, because of his penchant for middle-of-the-night horseback rides, during which he'd scream and shout. In 1904, he was committed to the state hospital and died seven years later. In 2015, workers excavating around his former home discovered six nude bodies with crushed skulls that had been discarded via a trapdoor inside the house. Five of the people were a family, killed all at once. No one has ever identified the victims, nor a motive for Butler, if he indeed killed them.

Eliot Ness attacked a homeless encampment to stop a killer.

After squaring off against Al Capone and other figures in the Chicago organized crime underworld, Eliot Ness became safety director for the city of Cleveland. In that role, he was tasked with figuring out who had killed twelve people and left their bodies—their limbs removed with surgical accuracy—in a creek bed off the Cuyahoga River. Because no one identified the victims, authorities determined that they were homeless people living in a Cleveland shantytown. Ness's solution: Burn the shantytown to the ground, forcing dispersal and a lack of victims for the serial killer. It worked—the killings stopped after Ness displaced the already displaced people.

The disappearance of Marvin A. Clark is the oldest cold missing persons case in the United States.

Marvin A. Clark left his home in suburban Tigard, Oregon, and arrived in downtown Portland via bus on October 30, 1926, to visit his daughter. He had no ID on his person, and he was never seen again, despite a large cash reward having been offered for clues to the seventy-five-year-old's whereabouts. In 1986, loggers working outside Portland discovered a full skeleton. A medical examiner determined the man died of a self-inflicted gunshot wound to the head. And then twenty-five years after that, Oregon's state forensic anthropologist sent a bone sample to the University of North Texas for DNA analysis. It wasn't Clark.

Philadelphia's "Boy in the Box" was identified after sixty-five years.

Philadelphia police almost didn't respond to a tip called in from a La Salle College student in February 1957 because it was so gruesome they thought it was a prank. It wasn't. The body of a child, around four years old, starved and covered in bruises, wrapped in a blanket, and placed in a cardboard box, was discovered in a wooded area. The case horrified and fascinated Philadelphians, who referred to the child as the Boy in the Box. Remains were exhumed for DNA testing in 1998, but his identity remained unknown until 2022, when Philadelphia police determined that the victim was four-year-old Joseph August Zarelli. His murderer and their motive remains a mystery in the active investigation.

A psychic was behind one of the earliest theories about the Boy in the Box.

Some initially thought that the Boy in the Box was a foster child who died accidentally by falling out of a window. The theory was first floated by Philadelphia medical examiner Remington Bristow, who was given this idea by a psychic. In 1961, Bristow visited the house the psychic indicated was the foster home in question, and verified that it was once a foster home. He also found a bassinet that would have shipped in the cardboard box that was used to store the Boy in the Box's remains.

JonBenét Ramsey was ransomed after she'd already died.

The sexual assault and murder of six-year-old child beauty queen JonBenét Ramsey on Christmas morning 1996 horrified and captivated the country. There are many quirks in the case, which made pinpointing a murderer and a motive nearly impossible, especially twenty-five years after the fact. Mother Patsy Ramsey awoke, couldn't find her daughter, and then discovered a handwritten, three-page ransom note demanding $118,000 for JonBenét's return. But by that point, the girl was already dead—slain and left in the basement of the home.

There were several major suspects in the death of JonBenét Ramsey.

Parents John and Patsy Ramsey emphatically and publicly denied having anything to do with their daughter's murder but Boulder, Colorado, police did look at them as suspects. One strange element in the case was that the Ramseys were very wealthy, so the $118,000 ransom seemed low. Other suspects included a homeless man, an electrician, a local Santa Claus portrayer, Ramsey's brother (who sued over the suggestion), and Mark John Karr, a convicted sex offender who falsely confessed.

A Massachusetts murder victim may have been spotted in *Jaws*.

The decomposed remains of a woman were found in sand dunes near Provincetown, Massachusetts, in July 1974. The deceased was lying on a beach towel. Her hands had been removed and replaced with piles of pine needles, her teeth were removed, and her clothes were folded beside her. Police failed to identify her, but a lead came in the 2010s, when author Joe Hill was watching *Jaws*, which was filmed in the Provincetown area in 1974, and spotted an extra who looked like a reconstructed image of "the Lady in the Dunes." Universal Pictures had no record of the extras from *Jaws*, however, and the woman remained unidentified.

A notorious serial criminal who terrorized Europe wasn't real.

From 1992 to 2008, law enforcement across Western Europe were baffled and frustrated by the activities of "the Phantom of Heilbronn." DNA samples obtained from six crime scenes linked the Phantom, who was believed at first to be a woman, to six murders and thirty crimes in Austria and Germany (including the death of a police officer in Heilbronn). In 2008, German police said they thought the Phantom might be a person born male, or possibly a transgender individual. In 2009, German authorities announced that the Phantom of Heilbronn didn't exist. All the common DNA was traced to a woman at the forensic swab factory who had unwittingly contaminated DNA evidence while gathering equipment.

Two women with the same name were murdered in the same week.

Two women in Texas were murdered in a similar fashion within days of each other in October 2000. One was a well-liked nurse; the other a well-liked loan officer. Both women were found dead in their cars. What linked them was their name: Mary Morris. Investigators never solved the case, but they believe that the husband of one Mary Morris ordered a hit on his wife, and the killer killed the wrong Mary Morris first, then the correct one.

CHAPTER 7

FALLEN STARS

Celebrities: They're just like
everybody else in that they're the
victims and perpetrators of some
very heinous crimes.

A major mystery author killed a friend's mother when she was a teenager.

Author Anne Perry has written more than a hundred detective novels set in historical time periods, many of them bestsellers and involving the characters William Monk and Thomas Pitt. "Anne Perry" is a pen name; the author's real name is Juliet Hulme. She changed it because, at age fifteen, she was involved in a salacious murder in New Zealand that was the basis for the 1994 Peter Jackson film *Heavenly Creatures*. In 1954, Hulme and her best friend Honorah Rieper killed Rieper's mother. She was tried as a minor and served five years in prison.

Two of the biggest names in weight lifting murdered their assistant, then failed to cover it up.

Craig Titus married fellow champion bodybuilder Kelly Ryan, and they hired Melissa James to be their assistant. In December 2005, James's charred corpse was discovered in Ryan's car in the desert outside of Las Vegas. Titus and Ryan fled and were arrested a week later in Boston. Their initial story: James died of a drug overdose, and, fearing they'd be implicated, they burned the body and left it in a car. That conflicted with evidence that James had been attacked with a stun gun, forced to take morphine, and strangled to death. Titus and Ryan were found guilty of murder.

The Beach Boys recorded a Charles Manson song.

Budding cult leader and wannabe rock star Charles Manson befriended Beach Boys drummer Dennis Wilson, who was so convinced that the future murderer had real talent that he tried to sign him to the band's label, Brother Records. He wrote a song just for the Beach Boys called "Cease to Exist," and the band recorded a demo of it. Under the direction of Wilson, the band later changed some of the words and melody, retitled it "Never Learn Not to Love," and released it as a B-side of the 1968 single "Bluebirds Over the Mountain." Within a year, Manson and his "family" had killed nine people.

When the Manson family killed a houseful of people in 1969, they were looking for a record producer who wronged the cult leader.

Dennis Wilson set up Charles Manson with record producer Terry Melcher. The son of screen legend Doris Day, Melcher had decided against signing Manson to a record contract after a poor audition. He still considered making a documentary about Manson, but called it off after seeing Manson get into a drunken fistfight. Melcher dropped all contact with Manson, which so angered him that in August 1969, he went to Melcher's home at 10050 Cielo Drive in Los Angeles to kill the producer. Melcher had moved out, and actor Sharon Tate was living there instead. Nevertheless, Manson and his followers killed all five people in the home that evening.

The musician who cowrote "Layla" killed his own mother.

Jim Gordon was one of the Los Angeles–based music industry's top session drummers in the 1960s and 1970s, playing on classic tracks by the Beach Boys, the Byrds, and George Harrison. When Eric Clapton formed the supergroup Derek and the Dominos, he hired Gordon to be the drummer. That band's biggest hit was the epic "Layla," which was cowritten by Gordon. Despite his musical prowess, he had severe mental health difficulties. Between 1978 and 1983, he sought treatment fifteen times, until, as he told police, he "snapped." He repeatedly stabbed his seventy-one-year-old mother until she was dead. When he was up for parole in 2018, his own attorney argued against Gordon being released, and he wasn't.

Music legend Sam Cooke was murdered in a motel after he was robbed.

Gospel star turned pop and R&B superstar Sam Cooke found his career, and life, cut short in December 1964. The thirty-three-year-old singer brought a woman back to a Los Angeles motel room, but she stole his stuff and ran off. Cooke confronted the motel's manager, Bertha Franklin, alleging that she and the thief must have been in cahoots. The fight turned physical, and Franklin shot Cooke, which she'd later claim was in self-defense. His last words were "Lady, you shot me!" There are holes in the story, however, with some investigators believing that Franklin was set up to shoot Cooke because he was part of the civil rights movement or had Mob ties.

Teenage Mark Wahlberg harassed and attacked a group of Black children.

Before he was an actor, Mark Wahlberg was a rapper under the name Marky Mark. Before that, as a teenager in the 1980s, he was a criminal. At age fifteen, and in the company of some older friends, Wahlberg chased three African American children and threw rocks at them while yelling racial slurs. Then Wahlberg did the same thing again the next day. He received a suspended sentence in 1986. Two years later, Wahlberg assaulted two men in what was classified as an anti-Vietnamese hate crime. One man he hit with a wooden stick; the other he punched in the face. Wahlberg pleaded guilty to felony assault and served forty-five days in jail.

Terrence Howard witnessed his father kill a man while waiting to see Santa.

Best known for his role on *Empire* and Oscar-nominated work in *Hustle & Flow*, actor Terrence Howard said that one of his earliest memories is of his father violently attacking a stranger. With his two brothers and parents, Howard went to Higbee's department store in Cleveland to see Santa Claus during the Christmas season of 1971. A man named John Fitzpatrick reportedly accused Tyrone Howard of cutting in line. An altercation broke out; Fitzpatrick allegedly kicked Howard in the groin, who retaliated by delivering multiple, fatal stab wounds with an unknown weapon. Tyrone Howard served just under a year in prison for what the local media dubbed "the Santa Line Slaying."

Days after knocking his team out of the World Cup, a soccer star was murdered in his hometown.

Going into the 1994 FIFA World Cup, pundits predicted that Colombia could make a deep run, thanks in part to star defender Andrés Escobar. Indeed, he was responsible for one of the tournament's most memorable moments—when he accidentally scored on his own goal, giving a win to the U.S., and leading to an early exit for Colombia. Less than a week later, after a night of partying in his hometown of Medellín, Colombia, Escobar was shot dead.

An early rap pioneer allegedly killed a man who he thought was making a pass at him.

As a member of Grandmaster Flash's Furious Five, Kidd Creole (a.k.a. Nathaniel Glover) was one of the first rap stars and was inducted into the Rock and Roll Hall of Fame. By summer 2017, he was working as a security guard in New York City, and on the way to his job, he ran into a man named John Jolly. Glover stabbed Jolly twice in the chest with a steak knife that he carried for protection. Glover ran to his place of business, discarded his bloodied clothes, and washed his knife. He was arrested a day later, and in 2022 was found guilty of manslaughter. Authorities alleged that Glover killed Jolly because he thought the man was coming on to him. Glover insisted he acted in self-defense.

The father of actor Woody Harrelson was a prolific contract killer.

Woody Harrelson—star of *Cheers*, *The Hunger Games*, and *Zombieland*—is the son of Charles Harrelson, a career criminal and con artist who died in a Colorado prison in 2007. Charles was believed to have been involved in (but never convicted of) dozens of deaths in the 1960s; he got out of prison in 1978 after serving time for being an accomplice to murder. The following year, U.S. District Judge John H. Wood was gunned down outside of his home in San Antonio. Drug dealer Jamiel Chagra was scheduled to go before the judge, but instead hired Harrelson to kill him.

The star of *Hogan's Heroes* was murdered with camera equipment.

After his long stint on the hit sitcom *Hogan's Heroes* ended in 1971, actor Bob Crane fell into obscurity, touring the country with dinner theater productions. In June 1978, another actor in one of those plays discovered Crane's dead body in his temporary apartment in Scottsdale, Arizona. Authorities ruled he'd been murdered, as an electrical cord was tied around his neck and he'd been bludgeoned to death with a camera tripod. His cause of death tipped authorities off about Crane's secret life. He'd been traveling the country with an electronics salesman, with whom he'd engaged in intimate joint encounters with women, and filmed them. No culprit was ever arrested.

A *Harry Potter* star died defending his brother in a bar fight.

Teen actor Rob Knox landed one big role in his career, a wizard student named Marcus Belby in *Harry Potter and the Half-Blood Prince*. He was supposed to appear in future franchise installments, but he died before filming began. In May 2008, Knox and his brother were at a pub in London when a knife-wielding stranger named Karl Bishop challenged them to a fight. He lunged at Knox's brother, and Knox tackled him. In the melee, he was stabbed four times and died of his wounds later that day at age eighteen. Bishop was sentenced to life in prison.

Natalie Wood drowned after a fight at sea with her husband.

West Side Story star Natalie Wood married fellow actor Robert Wagner, and in 1981, she partied with him and their friend Christopher Walken on the yacht the *Splendor* off the coast of Southern California. The captain heard the couple fighting (Wagner thought Wood was flirting with Walken), and at some point, Wood left the boat in a dinghy and tried to sail to land. Her body was found the next morning on Catalina Island. The coroner ruled her death an accidental drowning, but in 2011, the Los Angeles County Sheriff's Department reopened the case and edited Wood's death certificate so that the cause included "undetermined factors." Those factors: newly discovered evidence that Wood had been severely beaten before she hit the water, indicating she was thrown overboard.

A contestant from *The Voice* was killed by an obsessed fan.

The biggest musical success story to emerge from *The Voice*, NBC's long-running singing competition reality show, was Christina Grimmie, a powerful balladeer who notched several hit singles and went on a nationwide tour in 2016. During that run, Grimmie played a show in Orlando that included a paid meet-and-greet post-concert event. It was attended by a man named Kevin Loibl, a Grimmie fan who told coworkers that he knew the singer, that they were dating, and that they planned to get married. Instead, he shot Grimmie at the meet-and-greet. The singer's brother tackled him, but Loibl broke away and turned the gun on himself, dying instantly. Grimmie, twenty-two, died later that night.

O.J. Simpson wrote a book about how he hypothetically would have killed his ex-wife.

Acquitted in 1995 of the brutal murders of his former wife, Nicole Brown, and her friend Ron Goldman, despite a plethora of evidence, NFL and movie star O. J. Simpson has repeatedly attested to his innocence and promised to bring the actual culprit to justice. However, in 2006, Simpson coauthored a book called *If I Did It*, an extremely detailed, step-by-step hypothetical account of how Simpson says he *would* have committed the murders *had* he committed the murders. Due to public outcry, the book, and a tie-in TV special, were canceled before they were released.

A *Sons of Anarchy* star killed his landlady and her cat and then fell to his death.

Johnny Lewis landed roles on *Smallville*, *The O.C.*, *Malcolm in the Middle*, and *Sons of Anarchy* in the 2000s, departing the last show because he despised the onscreen violence. But that's when his real-life pattern of violence began. After being released from prison for assault in 2012, Lewis rented a room at a creative retreat owned and operated by eighty-one-year-old Cathy Davis. Police received a report of a woman screaming at the villa, and found Lewis dead on impact in the driveway when they arrived. It wasn't clear if he'd fallen or jumped off the building. Then police discovered Davis's body inside. She had died of strangulation and blunt force trauma. Detectives believe Lewis beat Davis—as well as her cat—to death before he died.

A deathrow inmate claimed credit for the murder of Nicole Brown Simpson.

In absence of a conviction for O. J. Simpson in the 1994 murders of Nicole Brown Simpson and Ron Goldman, a number of theories have been floated as to the identity of the true killer. If it wasn't Simpson, the culprit may have been Glen Rogers, who was on death row in Florida for a 1997 murder. He claims that O. J. Simpson hired him to kill Brown's drug dealer to eliminate her drug debts, but he botched the plan and he wound up killing Brown and Goldman instead. Others think those very drug dealers may have killed Brown over her supposed debts, a theory Simpson shared with prison guards.

A sitcom star died after answering her door.

Rebecca Schaeffer, the twenty-one-year-old star of the hit CBS sitcom *My Sister Sam*, was the obsession of a man named Robert Bardo, who hired a private investigator to find Schaeffer's address in Los Angeles. In 1989, he went to her home and shot Schaeffer on her doorstep. She repeatedly asked "Why?" as she bled to death.

Robert Bardo was originally obsessed with singer Debbie Gibson.

Robert Bardo became fixated on pop star Debbie Gibson, but after watching Rebecca Schaeffer in the 1989 movie *Scenes from the Class Struggle in Beverly Hills*, he turned his attention to her. Bardo was enraged that the actress had appeared in a sex scene, damaging her purity. He showed up at her house and shot her to death. Bardo was convicted and sentenced to life in prison, and the case led to the development of first-in-the-nation anti-stalking laws in California.

Rebecca Schaeffer's stalker tried to gain access to her years before he killed her.

From 1986 to 1988, model-turned-actress Rebecca Schaeffer starred on the hit CBS sitcom *My Sister Sam*. Almost immediately upon the show's debut, Robert Bardo developed an unhealthy obsession with Schaeffer, writing her multiple fan letters and, in 1987, visiting the set of *My Sister Sam*. But he was barred entry by security guards twice, the second time because he was found with a knife on his person.

A Seattle rock star was murdered by a man who wasn't convicted for more than a decade.

The Gits were one of many Seattle grunge bands that got attention after Pearl Jam and Nirvana broke out big in the early 1990s. Led by singer Mia Zapata, the Gits recorded a song for their second album called "Sign of the Crab," told from the point of view of a woman terrified of being murdered by a stranger. On July 7, 1993, Zapata left a Seattle bar and was brutally attacked by a stranger, Jesus Mezquia, who beat, assaulted, and strangled the singer to death with a sweatshirt cord. Mezquia was convicted after DNA evidence linked him to the crime in 2004.

A very young and prominent voice actor was killed by her father.

Child actor Judith Barsi was best known for her voice work, playing characters in the 1980s animated movies *All Dogs Go to Heaven* and *The Land Before Time*. Both of those films hit theaters after Barsi died. Her father, Jozsef, was an alcoholic prone to violent rages who abused his daughter and her mother, threatening to kill them on occasion. In July 1988, he made good on the threat, shooting Barsi and her mother, and then setting the house on fire and shooting himself.

One of the world's top athletes killed his girlfriend because he thought she was a burglar.

Oscar Pistorius was born without a fibula bone in both of his legs. His legs were amputated from the knees down while he was an infant. Nevertheless, thanks to the use of high-tech, lightweight prostheses, he became one of the fastest (and most inspiring) sprinters in the world, taking a gold medal at the 2004 Paralympics just two years after he started running, and competing in the 2012 Summer Olympics. On Valentine's Day 2013, Pistorius thought he heard an intruder in his bathroom. He grabbed a gun, entered the dark room, and started firing. He'd killed his girlfriend, Reeva Steenkamp. In a seven-month trial, with prosecutors arguing he'd intentionally killed Steenkamp, a judge pronounced Pistorius guilty of the equivalent of manslaughter. On appeal, that became murder, and he was sentenced to at least fifteen years in prison.

An NBA player disappeared at sea, and his brother is a prominent suspect.

NBA player Brian Williams retired after the 1998–99 season (having just changed his name to Bison Dele to honor his Native American and African ancestry), and became a nomad. He would end up in the South Seas, where he learned to operate a boat (the *Hakuna Matata*) with plans to sail from Tahiti to Hawaii in the summer of 2002 with his brother Miles Dabord, girlfriend Serena Karlan, and captain Bertran Saldo. The boat disappeared, but somehow Dabord surfaced on dry land. He was arrested in Phoenix trying to buy gold with a check stolen from Dele. He made bail, drove to Mexico, and killed himself with an overdose of insulin. Dele, Karlan, and Saldo were never found, but authorities have floated the theory that Dabord killed them all and dumped their bodies into the ocean.

Nick Nolte has a criminal past.

Nick Nolte was one of Hollywood's top actors in the 1980s and 1990s, with a successful career that included an Oscar nomination for *The Prince of Tides* virtually bookended by two serious legal incidents. In September 2002, he was arrested for driving while highly intoxicated; police presumed he was under the influence of alcohol, but tests revealed the substance to be the narcotic GHB. He pleaded no contest and received three years' probation. Back in 1965, Nolte was arrested for selling counterfeit draft cards during the Vietnam War. He evaded a possible forty-five-year prison sentence.

A dangerous drug cocktail led to the death of Phil Hartman.

Saturday Night Live and *The Simpsons* star Phil Hartman was murdered while he slept in his Los Angeles home in May 1998. He was shot by his wife, Brynn Hartman, who then killed herself. Their marriage had long been tumultuous, but what caused Mrs. Hartman to kill was a combination of severe clinical depression and an adverse chemical reaction. She'd quit drinking and had given up cocaine years before, but she had just started using them again. A coroner's report noted high amounts of those illicit substances in Hartman's bloodstream, along with a dose of a common antidepressant. When combined, cocaine, alcohol, and antidepressants can cause a panicked, manic, hopeless state.

Tupac Shakur survived a murder attempt two years before his death.

Rapper and actor Tupac Shakur was shot and killed while sitting in a car in Las Vegas in 1996, just two years after he survived another attempt on his life. While in the lobby of a recording studio in New York City, gunmen shot the entertainer five times. Shakur believed the whole thing was a setup, and not a random robbery, because the culprits didn't take his prominent Rolex watch. Nearly twenty years later, in 2011, shooter Dexter Isaac came forward as one of the recording studio assailants, and revealed that Shakur's disgruntled former agent James Rosemond had hired him to pull off the attack.

Sid Vicious's bodyguard claimed to have killed his client's girlfriend.

Sex Pistols guitarist Sid Vicious kept up a violent, drug-addled relationship with girlfriend Nancy Spungeon until she was found stabbed to death at New York's Hotel Chelsea in 1978. Vicious was the chief suspect. He even confessed to the murder, only to recant and then die of a heroin overdose before his trial. He was so high on barbiturates at the time of Spungeon's murder that he believed he killed her without having any memory of the incident. To add even more of a twist, Rockets Redglare, Vicious's bodyguard and drug supplier, frequently confessed to the murder to friends, but they didn't believe he did it.

AC/DC's drummer allegedly tried to hire a hit man.

For most of the years spanning 1975 to 2015, Phil Rudd played drums for the enormously successful hard rock band AC/DC. One of their best-known songs is "Dirty Deeds Done Dirt Cheap," about a wily hit man offering his professional killing services. The song became a hit in 1976. Fast forward to 2015: Rudd pleaded guilty to threatening to kill a former assistant. According to court records, he offered cash, cars, and a house to an associate after asking to have the former assistant "taken out." For that crime and for possession of methamphetamine and marijuana, he was sentenced to eight months of house arrest.

The last photos of John Lennon include his assassin.

At about 4 P.M. on the afternoon of December 8, 1980, rock star and ex-Beatle John Lennon left his apartment in New York City's Dakota building, where he walked past a crowd of hard-core fans who often waited outside for a glimpse of their idol. Among them was photographer Paul Goresh, who snapped a few pictures of Lennon while he signed an album for a man who had approached him. Those would be the last photos taken of Lennon, and the man whose record he signed was Mark David Chapman, the man who would shoot and kill Lennon a few hours later when he returned to the Dakota.

Before he shot John Lennon, Mark David Chapman unnerved another rock star.

Mark David Chapman planned his assassination of John Lennon for two months, moving to New York to commit the murder. On the day before shooting Lennon, Chapman accosted another rock star, James Taylor, a close friend of Lennon who lived in the apartment building next door to Lennon's Dakota. At a subway stop, a sweaty, frantic Chapman pinned James Taylor to the wall and told him that he was going to "get in touch" with Lennon. The next day, Taylor heard the gunshots that killed Lennon.

A Food Network host attempted to get two homeless men to murder his spouse.

Pastry chef Juan-Carlos Cruz hosted the 2000s Food Network show *Calorie Commando*, on which he shared his tips for making the healthy meals he'd eaten on the way to losing a hundred pounds. In May 2010, he was arrested in Santa Monica, California, after offering two homeless men $500 to kill his wife. One of the would-be hit men reported it to police and arranged a sting where Cruz delivered instructions on the contract killing. He was arrested, pleaded no contest to solicitation of murder, and served nine years in prison.

A Food Network reality show contestant abused and killed a foster child.

South Carolina resident Ariel Robinson won her season of Food Network's *Worst Cooks in America* contest. Six months after winning $25,000, she and husband Jerry Robinson were arrested and charged with homicide by child abuse. The couple had been foster parents of three-year-old Victoria Smith, who died in 2021 in their care, with a coroner's report attributing the cause of death to deadly blows with a blunt object. Robinson said the child died because she drank too much water. A jury deliberated for only an hour before finding Robinson guilty and handing her a life sentence.

Before he was a boxing promoter, Don King violently killed a man.

Don King is best known as a wild-haired boxing promoter, hyping fights and fighters in the 1970s and 1980s, most famously Mike Tyson, Joe Frazier, and Muhammad Ali. What most people don't know is that he had a checkered past. In the mid-1960s, he ran an illegal gambling parlor in Cleveland, and when a man refused to pay up on a $600 debt, King stomped on the man until he was dead. He was found guilty of second-degree murder, which was later reduced to manslaughter, and served a four-year prison sentence.

A Grammy Award winner survived a carjacking and being shot in the head.

Singer-songwriter Marc Cohn, winner of the Grammy Award for Best New Artist in 1992, was on tour in Denver in 2005 when a man approached his band's van and attempted to carjack it. Cohn and the driver, tour manager Thomas Dube, wouldn't give up the van, and the attacker fired his gun. The bullet grazed Dube and entered Cohn's temple. Dube was quickly treated and released, and Cohn went home after just two days, baffling doctors, who had not expected him to survive being shot in the head.

Fran Drescher changed the way TV shows are taped because of a vicious assault.

In 1985, future star Fran Drescher experienced a home invasion when the apartment she shared with her then-husband was broken into by two gun-wielding robbers. One of the men burgled the home, while the other sexually assaulted Drescher and a friend. When Drescher developed her sitcom *The Nanny* for CBS in the early 1990s, she was still coping with fear and anxiety over the attack. She persuaded the network to screen the studio audience for tapings, hiring extras instead of random people off the street. That's a safety measure that changed how TV shows are made.

A stalker pretended to be associated with a famous filmmaker to gain access to actor Theresa Saldana.

Theresa Saldana's breakout role was in the 1980 movie *Raging Bull*, directed by Martin Scorsese. Scotland-born homeless man Arthur Richard Jackson grew obsessed with Saldana after seeing *Raging Bull* and, having found her phone number via a private investigator, called the actress pretending to be Scorsese's assistant and asked for her home address in regards to a future role. Jackson then met Saldana at her home, and he stabbed her with a hunting knife, puncturing her lung. A deliveryman who heard Saldana's cries for help incapacitated Jackson, but Saldana was severely injured and spent four months in the hospital. She went on to become a victims' rights advocate.

Singer Selena was murdered by a friend, business associate, and superfan.

Tejano music superstar Selena was set to break through into the English language market in 1995 when she was murdered at age twenty-three. Her killer: Yolanda Saldivar, a fan so obsessive she lobbied Selena's father to start a fan club, then became president of it and ended up managing Selena's clothing boutiques. She was an erratic boss who fired people at will and embezzled more than $30,000 from both businesses by check forgery. Selena and her father confronted Saldivar and demanded some financial records. Saldivar was angry, but arranged to meet Selena at a Texas motel to review the financial records. It was at the Corpus Christi Days Inn that Saldivar shot Selena in the back, hitting a major artery and causing fatal blood loss and death. Saldivar turned herself in after a nine-hour standoff with authorities.

Robert Kennedy's support for Israel led to his murder on the campaign trail.

The ongoing dispute between Israelis and Palestinians manifested in violence against an American politician for the first time in 1968. Presidential candidate Robert Kennedy spoke at the Ambassador Hotel in Los Angeles. Afterward, while exiting through the kitchen, he was shot and killed by Sirhan Sirhan, a Palestinian man who was motivated to kill the politician solely because he publicly sided with Israel. The gunman was quickly subdued after the shooting by several prominent figures, including football star Rosey Grier and Olympic gold medalist Rafer Johnson.

Contrary to police belief, Sal Mineo died in a random attack.

Sal Mineo, an Academy Award–nominated teen idol for the 1955 film *Rebel Without a Cause*, saw his career fade by the 1970s after he became one of the first celebrities to announce he was part of the LGBT community. In 1976, he was stabbed by a mugger outside his apartment in West Hollywood, and he died within minutes. Police thought Mineo might have had ties to the criminal underworld that prompted the attack. That changed in 1978, when police in Michigan arrested a bad-check writer named Lionel Williams, overheard bragging to other criminals that he'd killed Mineo. He later recanted, but police still linked him to the crime, for which he received a fifty-year prison sentence.

The parents of the man who killed Gianni Versace tried to make the murder seem like a Mob hit.

When the body of Gianni Versace was found outside his home, shot and killed on a Miami street, a dead bird lay next to the body. That's a calling card of some Mafia organizations, leading to a theory that Versace, born in Italy, had been ordered killed by an Italian criminal family. Further investigation showed that a fragment of the bullet fired by Andrew Cunanan had clipped and killed the bird.

The Mafia connection rumor was actually floated and spread by Cunanan's parents to divert attention away from their son.

Andrew Cunanan could have been captured earlier, with better record-keeping.

After killing four people, including real estate developer Lee Miglin in 1997, Andrew Cunanan fled to Miami. The FBI had no idea where he was for months, despite him leaving numerous clues as to his whereabouts. He stole a valuable coin from Miglin, then sold it to a pawnshop in Miami; the store took Cunanan's full name, last known address, thumbprints, and a copy of his passport. An officer had looked at those records, but during the week in July 1997, when Cunanan killed fashion designer Gianni Versace (whom he'd met once in passing), that officer was on vacation, and none of his colleagues knew he'd had the information.

Lana Turner's daughter killed her mother's boyfriend (and then they were sued).

Golden Age of Hollywood star Lana Turner dated Johnny Stompanato, an enforcer and bodyguard for Mickey Cohen's crime family in the late 1950s. In the spring of 1958, just after the couple returned from a Mexican vacation, Turner's fourteen-year-old daughter, Cheryl Crane, stabbed Stompanato to death in her mother's bedroom, an act of retaliation for him beating her mother. A coroner's ruling called it justifiable homicide, and Crane avoided prosecution, although Stompanato's family later sued Turner for $750,000, settling for $20,000.

An unsolved murder was linked to a famous murder six decades later.

The Walker family of Osprey, Florida, was murdered during a home invasion in December 1959. The perpetrator left very little evidence—a bloody bootprint and a single fingerprint on a faucet. More than five hundred suspects were pursued, but no charges were ever filed. More than sixty years later, the Sarasota County Sheriff's Office received a tip that the Walker murders were connected to the Clutter family deaths, the subject of Truman Capote's 1966 true crime classic *In Cold Blood*. The home invasion and murders were nearly identical in their execution, and they occurred within a month of each other. But as Perry Smith and Dick Hickock had been executed in 1965 for the Clutter deaths, there was no way to try them or to confirm the connection.

CHAPTER 8

WORLD OF CRIME

The United States may be the
unofficial headquarters of true
crime, but murder, assault, and other
terrifying attacks happen all
over the world.

Anonymous witnesses claim an Australian murderer was only the fall guy for a secret organization.

In 1984, Adelaide, Australia, accountant Bevan Spencer von Einem was convicted of committing one out of five connected murders of teenage boys and young men in the area between 1979 and 1983. He's believed to have participated in all the murders, but prosecutors couldn't prove it. Anonymous, threatened witnesses told police that Von Einem hadn't acted alone, and was part of a shadowy cabal of wealthy elites called "the Family," which collectively preyed on young men. No further arrests were made, not after the witnesses' revelations nor in 2008, after the case was reopened by Adelaide police.

A Russian hypnotist successfully robbed a series of Moldovan banks.

In 2005, police in Moldova pursued a serial bank robber who was able to make off with more than the equivalent of $40,000 in his crime spree. Identified as Vladimir Kozak, he was a trained hypnotist from Russia. His M.O.: He'd start talking to a bank teller and then make eye contact, immediately putting the teller into a trance so deep they'd robotically oblige when he told them to hand over all the cash on hand. Wanted posters with Kozak's face went up around the nation, but police advised bank clerks not to look directly at it.

A heavy metal musician whose music celebrated murder was killed by a bandmate.

Heavy metal musician Oystein Aarseth helped create the Norwegian black metal scene in the 1980s under the stage name "Euronymous." His band, Mayhem, along with a few other bands, made music that advocated killing, chaos, mass destruction, and Satan worship. In 1992, a member of the Norwegian black metal scene named Varg Vikernes played bass for Mayhem. In 1993, Vikernes got into an argument with Aarseth and stabbed him to death. He received a prison sentence of twenty-one years, the longest sentence permitted by Norwegian law.

A discovery of an archaeological artifact tricked a killer into confessing.

Police believed that Peter Reyn-Bardt killed his wife, Malike de Fernandez, but they had no evidence—until 1983 when a skull was uncovered in a peat bog near Reyn-Bardt's house. The discovery of the skull awakened Reyn-Bardt's guilty conscience. Convinced it was that of his victim, he confessed to murdering de Fernandez and disposing of her dismembered remains into the bog. That fueled his conviction, but the skull wasn't actually that of his wife. Forensic testing showed that it belonged to a woman who'd died in the bog more than 1,700 years earlier.

The youngest convicted murderer in Canada led to the abolition of the death penalty in Canada.

In 1959, fourteen-year-old Steven Truscott gave twelve-year-old Clinton, Ontario, classmate Lynne Harper a ride on his bike. Two days later, Harper's murdered body was found, and because Truscott was the last person to see her alive, he became the chief suspect. After a two-week trial, Truscott was found guilty and sentenced to death by hanging, the youngest person to ever get that punishment in Canada. He received a stay of execution, and his sentence was later commuted to life. In 1969, he was paroled; in 1976, Canada did away with the death penalty altogether owing to the severe consequences of such a botched case.

Gordon Ramsay's TV show was derailed by a Costa Rican cabal.

TV food personality and chef Gordon Ramsay is an outspoken critic of illegal shark fishing, the subject of his BBC documentary *Gordon's Shark Bait*. For the film, he went to Costa Rica to expose a shady network of shark fin traders. That cabal, which has ties to drug trafficking cartels, tried to stop Ramsay and his crew, ambushing them at gunpoint and pouring gasoline on them. The police couldn't do anything. They recommended that Ramsay and his crew immediately leave Costa Rica.

A cannibalistic serial killer wouldn't eat overweight people.

From 1997 to 1999, Dorangel Vargas lived as a homeless person on the streets of San Cristóbal, Venezuela, and he stalked eleven men in a city park, killing them and then eating their flesh. After his arrest and imprisonment, he came to be known as el Comegente, or the People Eater, but he wasn't indiscriminate in his cannibalism. He would only kill and eat men, not women, because he said their flesh tasted better. Furthermore, he wouldn't eat overweight people, claiming the high cholesterol was bad for him.

During World War II, a woman killed and made soap to save her son from the fighting.

From 1939 to 1940, Leonarda Cianciulli murdered three women in the Italian village of Correggio, disposing of the bodies by melting the fat and using it as the basis of soap, then turning other parts into tea cakes. Her victims didn't particularly wrong Cianciulli in any way; she chose them as a sacrifice. With World War II underway in Europe, Cianciulli thought that if she appeased God in such a way, her son would be kept out of deadly combat.

A Russian murderer was hard to catch because of a rare and strange DNA disorder.

At least fifty-two assaults, murders, and mutilations of women and children can be attributed to the Butcher of Rostov—also known as the Rostov Ripper, the Red Ripper, and Andrei Chikatilo—who terrorized Russia, Ukraine, and Uzbekistan from 1978 to 1990. He was especially hard to find because even though he left extensive DNA evidence behind each time, in the form of blood and semen traces, he had a rare genetic condition in which the DNA in those two bodily fluids didn't match.

Robert Maudsley killed more people in prison than outside of it.

Robert Maudsley spent most of his childhood in an orphanage, where he was sexually abused. While working as a prostitute in 1973, Maudsley was picked up by a laborer named John Farrell, who showed him images he'd taken of a girl he'd abused. It enraged Maudsley enough that he slowly choked the man to death with a wire and then smashed his skull with a hammer. After being sent to Broadmoore Hospital in Berkshire, England, in 1977, he and another patient tied up and tortured for ten hours a pedophile named David Francis. On July 28, 1978, after being transferred to Wakefield Prison, he committed two murders in one day. From that point on, he was sent to live in a specially built solitary confinement unit.

Japanese organized crime syndicates loom large in big business.

Yakuza, the term for Japanese organized crime units, are entrenched in the Japanese economy. They've historically practiced *sokaiya*, or large-scale bribery. An organization will buy enough shares of a company to get a prominent seat on the shareholders board, then threaten to expose secrets of the company brass in exchange for a bribe. Sokaiya had become endemic by 1982, so Japan made it illegal for corporations to pay off blackmailers, forcing yakuza to be more secretive with it. Today, to avoid yakuza making a scene at company meetings, 90 percent of publicly held Japanese corporations hold their shareholder meetings on the same day each year. The government also introduced fines to businesses that knowingly cooperate with yakuza groups.

The fastest rescue operations in Japan are yakuza-run.

When a tsunami devastated Japan in 2011, yakuza organizations were the fastest and most generous with relief and aid. This was also the case after a 1995 earthquake in Kobe, when they used boats and helicopters to deliver supplies and food around the impassable streets. After the disasters, the yakuza then vied for construction contracts.

A fraud case carried the longest prison sentence ever.

Corporate fraud—or "swindling the public," as it's called in the Thailand legal system—is a very serious matter. In 1989, Chamoy Thipyaso was found guilty of the crime after swindling $204 million out of 16,000 people in a pyramid scheme. She garnered the longest prison sentence in history: 141,078 years.

A kidnapped child was watched over by lions.

In 2005, criminals in Ethiopia kidnapped a twelve-year-old and fled, after which they encountered a pride of lions. The kidnappers abandoned the child with the ferocious beasts, which, for whatever reason, left the kid alone. The pride seemed to be protecting the girl, settling in proximity to her. The kidnappers were caught, and the girl was returned home safely.

A Greek thief boldly agitated the military and police.

Vassillis Palaiokostas stole a tank from the Greek military in 1990, then used it to break his brother out of jail. It wasn't the first time he acted big. He also once blockaded a police station so that he could rob a jewelry store—the police were so well barricaded that they couldn't get out of their HQ to stop or arrest him.

A Canadian Zambian doctor hid blood to trick DNA tests.

Born in Zambia and practicing in Canada, Dr. John Schneeberger dogged and sexually assaulted many of his female patients (as well as his stepdaughter) in the 1990s. He avoided arrest and capture by fooling DNA tests. DNA samples left on his victims didn't match the blood that was drawn from Schneeberger when he readily sat for blood extractions—because he had surgically implanted a tube of somebody else's blood in his arm.

A murderer in Japan stayed at the site of his slayings for hours afterward.

It's highly unusual for a murderer to stay behind at the scene of the crime—it increases the likelihood of capture and leaves behind more evidence as to their identity. That's what's so bizarre about the Setagaya family murder. On December 30, 2000, an assailant invaded the Miyazawa family home in the Setagaya neighborhood of Tokyo. Parents Mikio and Yasuko and children Rei and Niina were murdered. Afterward, the murderer stayed in the house for hours, eating food out of the refrigerator, taking a nap on the couch, and surfing the internet on the family computer. DNA evidence was recovered, but no arrest has ever been made.

A workboat in Poland discovered a balloon made of human skin.

One morning in January 1999, a tugboat operator identified only as "Miroslaw M." was working the Vistula River in Poland, unsticking his boat's propeller. He found a beige-colored sack that smelled horrible, and he couldn't determine what it was, until he noticed what looked like a human ear. He reported it to authorities, and the object was identified as the remains of missing Krakow college student Kataryzna Zowada. The thing stuck in the boat propeller was her entire skin, cut away and fashioned into a suit-like balloon.

A tiny piece of fabric led police to the location of a murder victim's death.

A lot of evidence was uncovered from Kataryzna Zowada's skin. DNA belonging to someone other than Zowada was isolated, tested, and compared to a national database of sexual offenders and persons of interests, but no match was made. The case went cold, only for Krakow police to reopen it in 2012, at which point traces of rare plants were found on the shred of sweater that remained on the skin, pinpointing the location of Zowada's death. Still, no arrests or suspect identifications have been made.

A man convinced a child that he was a werewolf, and that she should help him kill.

Jasmine Richardson was released from prison in 2016 after serving a ten-year sentence for assisting in the murder of her parents and younger brother in Medicine Hat, Alberta, Canada. Just twelve years old at the time, she'd committed the killings with her much-older boyfriend, twenty-three-year-old Jeremy Steinke, who had convinced Richardson that he was a three-hundred-year-old werewolf.

A prominent primate researcher was murdered in Rwanda, perhaps in retaliation.

Primate researcher, conservationist, and *Gorillas in the Mist* author Dian Fossey died in 1985, found bludgeoned to death in her cabin in the mountains of Rwanda. Fossey's assistant, Wayne McGuire, was convicted of the murder, with prosecutors alleging that he planned to steal Fossey's next book manuscript. He was sent back home to the U.S. and proclaimed his innocence. Other theories as to who really killed Fossey: someone connected to gorilla poachers, whom Fossey would routinely kidnap, torture, and interrogate.

A trio of Brazilian killers turned their victims into a profitable meat pie business.

Brazilian authorities arrested and charged Isabel Cristina Pires; her husband, Jorge Beltrao Negromonte da Silveira; and his mistress, Bruna Cristina Oliveira da Silva in 2012 for the kidnapping and murder of three women, including a homeless teenager. They disposed of the bodies by dismembering them, removing and cooking the flesh with salt and cumin, and making pies from it. Most were sold to neighbors, schools, and hospitals, while the trio ate most of them themselves, believing that doing so would purify their souls.

The Gruber family's murderer hid on their property for months beforehand.

The Gruber family—parents Andreas and Camilla, daughter Viktoria, her children, and a recently hired housekeeper—were murdered on the night of March 31, 1922, at their rural, isolated farm in what's now Waidhofen in the Bavaria region of Germany. An autopsy determined that all had been brutally murdered by a mattock, a handheld farm implement outfitted with a blade and a chisel. The murder remains unsolved more than a century later, although authorities do know *how* the killer did it. Footprints in the snow leading to the farm and attic, but not out of it, indicate that the killer hid in the attic of the Gruber's farmhouse for as long as six months before the murders.

The Gruber family's murderer stayed for days after killing them.

Whoever killed the Gruber family remained on their property after the murders. He or she stayed for four days, making sure to feed the cows, and eating all the bread out of the Grubers' pantry. Police had difficulty gathering evidence because the sensationalized crime attracted curious onlookers who contaminated the crime scene by entering and taking souvenirs. One crime-curious person even cooked a meal in the kitchen.

A gambler in Macau killed his creditor and then stole his restaurant.

Macau is a colony on mainland China that serves as the Las Vegas of Asia. The Eight Immortals was a hotel and restaurant complex there. The restaurant's owner, Zheng Lin, won a late-night bet against a criminal on the run named Huang Zhiheng, but was unable to collect on it for a year. Fed up, Zheng got angry and demanded his money after closing the restaurant one night, sending Huang into a rage. He took one of Zheng's sons hostage with a piece of broken glass and made the rest of the family restrain one another. Zheng's wife, Chen Huiyi, tried to run, and Huang stabbed her in the neck. Before the night was over, he'd killed ten people in the restaurant, primarily relatives of Zheng. After disposing of the bodies, he took over operations of the Eight Immortals restaurant as if nothing had happened.

A man from Brazil killed a lot of people, but only "bad" people.

Brazilian criminal Pedro Rodrigues Filho, a.k.a. Killer Petey, murdered a lot of people, but he did so with purpose. He was driven to kill only drug dealers, sex offenders, and other murderers. He was sent to prison in 1973 for a years-long killing spree that began when he was a teenager. According to authorities, his actions left seventy-one people dead. However, Filho took credit for more than a hundred.

Brazilian prison sentencing limits make for a lot of incarceration murders.

The Brazilian criminal justice system has a strict sentence-limiting law—no matter the extent or volume of the crimes committed, an individual can only serve a maximum of thirty years in one stretch. That meant convicted Brazilian serial and spree killer Pedro Rodrigues Filho wouldn't face much recompense if he continued his murderous purge of criminals in prison—which was quite full of people who did what he considered punishable by death. Before his release from prison in 2007, Filho murdered forty people behind bars, including the entire gang that killed his girlfriend. He also killed his father, because he had killed Filho's mother.

A murderous cannibal became a celebrity in his home country.

Paris police detained Japanese national Issei Sagawa after catching him in a park in 1981 with a suitcase that contained the remains of Renée Hartevelt. Sagawa had shot and killed Hartevelt three days earlier, then partially consumed him. Sagawa was sentenced to five years in a mental institution, after which he returned to Japan, where he reportedly didn't kill again but became a celebrity. In several film and TV re-creations of Sagawa's crimes, he played himself.

An Australian kidnapping victim was just over at her boyfriend's house for years.

Around the time that Leonard Fraser, known as "the Rockhampton Rapist," was active in Rockhampton, Australia, in 1998, fourteen-year-old Natasha Ryan disappeared. In a secretly recorded jailhouse confession in 2002, Fraser confessed to four murders, including Ryan's, whose remains or whereabouts were never determined. Fraser was tried and imprisoned for the crime, but then Rockhampton police, acting on a tip, raided the home of Scott Black. There they found Ryan hiding in a wardrobe. She'd been laying low at her boyfriend's home, two miles from her parents' house, for four years.

Very few murders have ever taken place in the Arctic Circle.

In 1970, a man named Porky Leavitt broke into a friend's trailer to steal his stash of raisin wine. But the friend caught Leavitt in the act, and he shot him dead with a rifle blast. This is one of the few violent crimes to ever go down in the Arctic Circle, and the only murder ever on Fletcher's Ice Island, an iceberg.

A major theft of Van Gogh artworks was botched because of a flat tire.

Amsterdam's Van Gogh Museum is home to many of the traditional master artist's works, and in April 1991, twenty of those paintings disappeared in a well-planned but poorly executed art heist. A team of four Dutch men (including one of the museum's security guards) roamed around the museum at 3 A.M. and picked out the artworks they wanted to take, then loaded them into a guard's car. They drove off in the getaway vehicle, got a flat tire soon after, and left the car—with the paintings inside—so they wouldn't be caught with the stolen masterworks. Authorities recovered the paintings in thirty-five minutes and had arrested all four men within three months.

Chocolates and flirting got a man entry into a diamond vault.

Carlos Flomenbaum spent a year kissing up to the staff of ABN Amro Bank in Antwerp, Belgium, complimenting employees on their looks and providing regular gifts of high-end chocolates. Eventually he talked someone into giving him VIP access that allowed him access to the vault. One weekend in March 2007, Flomenbaum entered that vault and walked away with $28 million worth of diamonds.

A Filipino politician cracked his own murder case.

Reynaldo Dagsa was a politician in the Philippines who served on a peacekeeping team and on a major council. At the stroke of midnight on New Year's Eve, when 2011 became 2012, Dagsa was killed by an assassin who timed his gunshots so that they'd be drowned out by the loud fireworks going off in the sky. Dagsa had his camera out to take pictures of those fireworks, and before he died, he managed to take a photo of his murderer. His photos led police to arrest his murderer within a week.

A random commuter thwarted a million-dollar armored truck heist in London.

A group of criminals orchestrated a heist in South London in February 2000, zooming across a road and screeching to a halt to box in an armored car transporting £10 million in cash. Then a fourth vehicle arrived, containing the battering ram–like spike needed to break into the money truck. While setting up the implement of destruction, the thieves left the van carrying it unattended, allowing a passing motorist and witness to sneak in and pull the keys out of the ignition. Stymied, the thieves set the spike car on fire and were eventually caught while planning a heist on a diamond exhibition at the Millennium Dome.

A boy in China held himself for ransom.

A boy named Yang was kidnapped from his home in Shangqiu, China, in 2008, with captors demanding 10,000 yuan for the kid's safe release. Yang's parents agreed to pay that amount (the equivalent of about $1,400), only for the kidnappers to demand the money be placed onto a debit card. Police then monitored area ATMs to look out for the kidnappers using that card, and instead they found Yang. He'd staged the kidnapping himself, attempting to bilk his parents out of the money he'd need to buy himself a new video game console.

A man in Hong Kong killed two people with a toxic yoga ball.

In May 2015, a jogger spotted two obviously dead women slumped over in a parked car in Hong Kong. Police identified the deceased, a forty-seven-year-old mother and her sixteen-year-old daughter, but found the doors locked and no signs of struggle. An autopsy showed that the two died of carbon monoxide poisoning, but there were no leaks in the car. Then they cracked the case: anaesthesiology professor Khaw Kim Sun, the woman's husband and the girl's father, had placed an inflatable yoga ball, filled with deadly carbon monoxide, in the trunk. He purposely didn't seal it, allowing the gas to slowly seep into the cabin of the car and kill them.

A serial killer in Hong Kong was caught because he got photos of his murders developed.

Only two serial killers have ever been identified in Hong Kong, and Lam Kor-wan was one of them. In the early 1980s, he worked as a taxi driver, a means to an end for finding victims. He'd pick up a female rider, drive somewhere remote, strangle her, and move the remains to his home, where he'd dismember her. His killing spree ended in 1982, when he sent a roll of film full of photos of dead bodies for processing at a Kodak lab.

Two employees at a Chinese bank had a good lottery ticket scheme going, until they overreached.

While working as a vault manager at the Agricultural Bank of China in 2007, Ren Xiaofeng devised a bold investment strategy: He'd steal 200,000 yuan (about $25,000) from his vault, use it to buy lottery tickets, then replace the money he'd stolen after he won. Despite near impossible odds, Ren won a fortune in that lottery, and a fraction of it he returned to the vault, nobody none the wiser. But then he tried to repeat the scheme, teaming up with another vault attendant to take thirty-two million yuan ($4.3 million) and spend most of it on lottery tickets. They didn't win that time, and they tried to cover their tracks with more lottery tickets purchased with an additional eighteen million in stolen yuan. The bank noticed, and had Ren and accomplice Ma Xiangjing arrested. They were executed for their crimes.

The crimes of two men in England revolved entirely around socks.

Steven Bain and Steven Gawthrop were apprehended and identified as the Southport Sockmen, two guys who would approach people in bars in Merseyside, England, in the mid-1990s and buy the socks they were wearing, claiming they were for a charity. It turns out Bain and Gawthrop were foot fetishists who derived great pleasure from socks; police found 10,000 socks in their residence, eighteen inches deep in some places. They went to prison and were assigned jobs in the prison laundry—as sock cleaners.

A vampiric killer actively looked forward to his execution.

Peter Kurten compiled an extensive criminal record of arson before becoming a rapist and murderer in 1929, the year he committed seven murders. Because the German killer sometimes drank his victims' blood, he was nicknamed "the Vampire of Dusseldorf." He was sentenced to death in 1931, and as prison officials placed his head under the guillotine's blade, he asked the psychiatrist present, "After my head is chopped off, will I still be able to hear, at least for a moment, the sound of my own blood gushing from the stump of my neck? That would be the pleasure to end all pleasures."

An unknown party used Japanese vending machines as a murder weapon.

Japan has more vending machines than anywhere else in the world, and they're used to sell all manner of wares. In 1985, this uniquely Japanese commerce system was part of a wave of fatal poisonings. The perpetrator would buy a bottled drink from a vending machine, inject it with a dose of the herbicide paraquat, then leave it right by the vending machine. An innocent, random customer would subsequently think they got lucky finding a free soda, only to ingest it and die. Ten people died that way, and the culprit was never identified.

CHAPTER 9

OLD TIMEY CRIMES

True crime is not a modern
phenomenon. For centuries, horrific
acts committed by others have
fascinated the populace.

One of the first identified serial killers in the United States did his deeds via a purpose-built hotel full of deadly traps.

In the 1890s, career conman Herman Webster Mudgett moved to Chicago, adopted the name Dr. H. H. Holmes, and built to his specifications a three-story building loaded with chutes, trapdoors, and tiny secret rooms. He rented out rooms to visitors of the 1893 Chicago World's Fair, and his house was perfect for ensnaring victims. Holmes would kill in one room, and then use his various devices to get their corpses to the basement for destruction in a kiln. By the time he was captured in 1894, Holmes had killed somewhere between twenty and two hundred people.

A controversial murder was immortalized in a Charles Dickens novel.

One of the grimmer parts of Charles Dickens's 1838 novel *Oliver Twist* is the violent murder of the character Nancy. When performing a live reading of the book, Dickens sometimes left out the death scene because it was just too soon after the murder of Eliza Grimwood, the inspiration for Nancy's fate. Grimwood's body was discovered with the throat slit, multiple postmortem stab wounds, and cuts all over, implying that she tried valiantly to fight off her assailant. There was a rumor at the time that a newspaper syndicate operated a death squad that committed brutal murders on slow news days so that their employer would have something to write about.

A Victorian woman argued that she bought a murderous level of arsenic as a beauty aid.

Emile L'Angelier and Madeleine Smith began a torrid affair in 1855—a forbidden love, as L'Angelier was working class and Smith a member of the elite upper crust. When Smith broke it off in favor of a gentleman of whom her family approved, L'Angelier attempted to blackmail her, but in 1857 he died of arsenic poisoning. Smith was tried for murder, but insisted that her purchase of a large quantity of arsenic shortly before L'Angelier's death was for her beauty routine. Victorian women *did* use arsenic to lighten their complexion. Smith was found not guilty.

The remains of Elizabeth Jackson washed up in the Thames River, piece by piece.

Three young boys were playing around the Thames River in the Battersea neighborhood of London in June 1889 when they discovered what was unmistakably a human thigh, cleanly detached at the hip and knee bones, with all the flesh intact. They delivered it to police, who decided that one surfaced body part wasn't enough to open an investigation. Then a box of flesh was found by a gardener, a torso was found in the Thames, an arm washed up, and over the span of a week, multiple organs, limbs, bones, and pieces turned up. Virtually the entire body of Elizabeth Jackson was reassembled, along with an undeveloped fetus. Who killed her and why? Nobody knows.

A silent-film director's incorrect manner of death was determined by a fake doctor.

William Desmond Taylor was a prolific filmmaker who directed dozens of silent movies. In 1922, his valet, Henry Peavey, discovered Taylor's dead body at his Los Angeles home. A crowd gathered, and from it emerged a man claiming to be a doctor, who ruled that a stomach hemorrhage had killed the director. But when the actual police showed up, they noticed a gunshot wound in Taylor's back. The "doctor" was nowhere to be found.

A Hungarian countess got away with killing and drinking the blood of dozens of victims.

Countess Elizabeth Báthory ruled over a region of Hungary in the early 1600s and committed unspeakable crimes against servants and peasants for years. The Blood Countess, as she was called, lived in a castle outfitted with a torture chamber where she'd hold girls kidnapped from nearby villages. She'd bite and swallow pieces of flesh from her still-living victims, shove needles under their fingernails, and then bleed them to death, drinking that blood because she believed it kept her appearance youthful. She made one victim cook and eat a piece of herself. It was only when Báthory stopped killing poor people in favor of nobles that anybody stood up to her. In 1611, she was put on trial, found guilty of eighty counts of murder, and locked in a room in her castle until she died three years later.

The word "thug," a violent miscreant, is derived from the name of a nineteenth-century killer.

Thug Behram is likely history's most prolific serial killer, as he's responsible for as many as 931 murders in central India between 1790 and 1840. His murder weapon of choice was a handkerchief fashioned into a garotte for choking. Only 125 of those deaths were confirmed to have been at the hands of Behram, but he also led a cult called thuggees, which robbed and killed tens of thousands of travelers. The name of his cult would later give way to the term "thug."

A New Orleans woman tortured her slaves so severely that other slaveholders opposed her actions.

Wealthy New Orleans landowner Delphine LaLaurie treated her slaves with remarkably sadistic cruelty. In 1833, she chased a slave child onto the roof of her mansion and whipped her until she fell off and died, then hid the body in a well. Police forced LaLaurie to sell off her remaining slaves, only for the madame to get her relatives to purchase them and bring them back to her home. One slave set Madame LaLaurie's mansion on fire in 1834 and escaped, leading authorities to the torture chamber in the attic, where beaten slaves were chained up and half-dead. This was too much even for other slaveholding landowners, who formed a mob and forced LaLaurie to flee to Paris.

A nineteenth-century nurse killed with the aim of being the most prolific murderer of all time.

While working as a nurse throughout New England in the late nineteenth century, Jane Toppan was the caregiver to thirty-one patients who died under her care. Suspicions only arose after four members of the Davis family, all treated by Toppan, died within weeks of one another in 1901. The husband of one of the dead called for an autopsy, which cited fatal levels of atropine and morphine as the cause of death. Toppan admitted that she'd killed all thirty-one people with those two substances. "That is my ambition, to have killed more people—more helpless people—than any man or woman who has ever lived," Toppan said during her trial. She was found guilty by way of insanity and lived out her days in an asylum.

More than a thousand witnesses couldn't determine the identity of Jack the Ripper.

Probably the most notorious unidentified serial killer of all time was Jack the Ripper, who brutally murdered and mutilated five sex workers in London in 1888. The case was closed in 1892, despite interviews with 1,500 witnesses turning up hundreds of possible suspects.

There's one suspect out of many who fits the description of Jack the Ripper.

Based on the profile created by London police and Scotland Yard, the person who was most likely the anonymous Jack the Ripper was a man named David Cohen, a.k.a. Nathan Kaminsky. Weeks after the last murder, he was picked up wandering the streets of London, muttering in Yiddish. He was taken to an asylum, where he attacked guards and other residents, refused to eat, and eventually died. When the Jack the Ripper murders occurred, Kaminsky was being treated for the maddening effects of syphilis near the Ripper's stalking ground. What's more suspicious is that when he was sent to the asylum, the murders ended.

Jack the Ripper killed two women with the same name.

On the evening of September 29, 1888, prostitute Catherine Eddowes was arrested by London police for public drunkenness. Just before 1 A.M., she'd sobered up enough to be released, and as she left, police recorded her name as the fake one she'd provided: Mary Kelly. A few hours later, she became Jack the Ripper's fourth victim. The fifth and final victim was also named Mary Kelly.

A doctor attempted to confess to Jack the Ripper's murders during his execution.

Thomas Neil Cream, a doctor from London, committed four murders in London in 1891 and 1892, poisoning four prostitutes. When Cream was in the middle of being executed, he shouted out, "I am Jack the—," but then the trapdoor of the gallows opened and Cream was hanged, his words cut off. Was he Jack the Ripper? It's not likely, as he was in Illinois—imprisoned for murder—during the peak of Jack the Ripper's killing era.

A gangster jokingly claimed that his mother killed him.

Arnold "the Brain" Rothstein was the brains of an organized criminal ring in New York in the 1920s, arranging the payouts, payoffs, and finances that allowed his cohort to run the underworld. In 1928, he played in a high-stakes poker game, arranged by George McManus, and lost $320,000. He refused to pay up, claiming the game was rigged. Weeks later, McManus offered to negotiate, in public and in safety, at the fancy Park Central Hotel. Rothstein was found in a stairwell, clutching his abdomen in pain. He died a day later from a gunshot wound. Police thought McManus was responsible, or one of the many other organized crime rivals that Rothstein had angered, but he refused to finger the accomplice. When repeatedly asked who shot him, Rothstein quipped, "Me mudder did it."

An urban legend about a vehicular intruder is based on a story from the 1830s.

There's an oft-repeated urban legend about a woman who leaves a mall, gets into her car, and finds a gentle, tired, old woman inside who requests a ride home. When the first woman remembers she'd locked her car, she goes back into the mall on an invented errand, and retrieves a security guard, who gets into a scuffle with the old woman—only to have her wig fall off and an ax drop from her bag. This is based on a true story about an event in England in 1834. A man finds an old woman in his carriage. He doesn't panic until he realizes she's wearing a wig and sees two pistols inside her handbag.

A twentieth-century murderer imitated the behavior of a gorilla.

Why was Earle Leonard Nelson, who murdered twenty-two boardinghouse landladies in the U.S. and Canada in 1926 and 1927, known as the Gorilla Killer? It's lost to history, but it's theorized that it's because he strangled his victims to death with the strength of a jungle beast. He also had a giant forehead, large lips, and large hands, which made him look like a gorilla. Plus, his aunt told detectives that after a childhood head trauma, Nelson was prone to manic periods during which he would walk around on his hands like a crazed ape.

Lizzie Borden escaped conviction on a technicality.

The murder trial of Sunday-school teacher Lizzie Borden was the most sensational courtroom ordeal of the late nineteenth century. In 1892, Andy and Abbie Borden were found murdered—hacked to pieces with an ax—in their home in Fall River, Massachusetts. The only suspect: Andy's thirty-two-year-old daughter, Lizzie. It seemed like an open-and-shut case because of the suspect's many mistakes. She claimed she'd been in the barn during the murders; police concluded the barn hadn't been touched in days. She said she'd removed her father's boots before his death; in crime scene photos, his boots are on. She'd also bought poison just before the murders. Borden was found not guilty, with the jury citing reasonable doubt—a side door was open so a stranger *could* have come in and randomly killed the Bordens.

A New Orleans killer didn't bring his own weapons to the crime scene.

A serial killer known as "the Axeman" stalked New Orleans from 1918 to 1919. He attacked at random, at night, and was linked to six murders and twelve nonfatal attacks, all on sleeping strangers. The nickname was something of a misnomer, because the Axeman didn't necessarily kill with an ax. He'd break into homes and use whatever sharp implement was on hand, which was only sometimes an ax.

A cleanup crew destroyed all evidence of a terrorist attack.

Around noon one day in September 1920, a horse-drawn cart parked near the U.S. Assay Office and the J. P. Morgan building on Wall Street. The cart then drove into a crowd, and a moment later, it blew up. More than three hundred people were injured, and thirty people died immediately in what police thought was an accident. A city crew cleaned up the scene, throwing away any and all physical evidence, stymieing local and federal agencies' efforts to solve the crime when they realized that it was an act of terrorism.

A 1920 Wall Street bombing may have had something to do with an anarchist collective.

The only real lead in the 1920 bombing on Wall Street was when a mailman discovered four flyers at the scene from the American Anarchist Fighters demanding political prisoners be released. They were similar to flyers found near bombings orchestrated by an Italian anarchist collective. The FBI thought associates of anarchist Luigi Galleani were behind it, but it couldn't be proved, and Galleani fled the country.

The timing of Bugsy Siegel's murder lined up with the seizure of his business hundreds of miles away.

Early twentieth-century organized crime figures Bugsy Siegel and Meyer Lansky were childhood friends who became teenage thugs together and built a business through bootlegging and gambling. Siegel would lead the building of Las Vegas's first luxury hotel and casino, the Flamingo, in 1946, with Mob money from Lansky and others. The budget ballooned to $6 million, so Siegel stole money to finish the job. In 1947, he was shot dead in Beverly Hills. At the exact same moment, three of Lansky's associates entered the Flamingo and told officials they were running the casino now. The Beverly Hills police concluded that Siegel's own men shot him.

The first American serial killers used rocks as their calling card.

Micajah Harpe and Wiley Harpe, "Big" and "Little" Harpe, respectively, emigrated from Scotland to the U.S. in 1759. At first, they started invading the homes of men who supported the overthrow of British crown rule in the colonies during the American Revolution. And then they started killing for fun. They left a bizarre signature element to their crimes. After killing their victims, they'd disembowel them, dispose of their organs, and replace them with rocks.

True crime literature dates back more than a century.

Horrific crimes are not a modern concept, and neither is the public's fascination with reading about them. Thomas Seccombe's *Lives of Twelve Bad Men: Original Studies of Eminent Scoundrels by Various Hands,* published in 1894, is cited as the first work of "true crime" media. Seccombe profiled the wicked and sickening deeds of twelve individuals in the (illustrated) book, with tales of crime dating back to the 1530s.

Five firefighters tried several times to kill a colleague they'd marked for death.

Michael Malloy was a firefighter in the Bronx who lost his job during the Great Depression, along with five firefighter friends. As Malloy was a depressed alcoholic, it seemed like his death wouldn't be investigated too heavily, so all five guys took out a life insurance policy on him without his knowledge. They tried killing him in various ways—with poison, drowning, freezing, vehicular assault—but nothing took until they gassed him with carbon monoxide. That's when police finally took notice; all five firefighters were executed in the electric chair.

A serial killer greatly misunderstood the meaning of a Latin legal phrase, to his own downfall.

In the 1940s, John George Haigh claimed to have killed nine people in the U.K., but he was only ever linked to six deaths. He was nicknamed "the Acid Bath Murderer," because he'd plunge his victims, shot or beaten to death, into a tub of sulfuric acid to dissolve their bodies and destroy evidence. Haigh confidently believed that he couldn't be convicted because of his genius method of corpse disposal—he understood the Latin legal phrase *corpus delicti* ("body of the crime") to mean "no body, no crime." It actually refers to how lawyers have to prove a crime occurred before a conviction can happen. Haigh was convicted and executed despite having dissolved his victims.

The Mob collaborated with the U.S. military during World War II.

In 1942, during World War II, the U.S. Armed Forces were enduring sabotage attempts on troop transports leaving New York City. They hired the services of Joseph "Socks" Lanza, Lucky Luciano, and Meyer Lansky to help them uncover espionage attempts and get to the root of the sabotage. Since the Mob controlled the docks and ports, they reported all suspicious behavior, even helping undercover Feds get union cards so they could patrol those very docks.

A stadium's worth of people came to watch the nineteenth-century execution of two murderous lovers.

Marie de Roux moved from her native Switzerland to England in the mid-nineteenth century to work as a household domestic. She entertained the attention of two suitors: Frederick Manning, whom she married, and Patrick O'Connor, whom she kept seeing in secret. After a promised inheritance windfall wasn't arriving quickly enough, Manning and de Roux decided to murder O'Connor and ransack his house. De Roux shot O'Connor in the back of the head during dinner, and Manning stabbed him with a chisel. Then they buried him under the hearth and added quicklime to make the body decompose faster. Their eventual trial was so sensationalized that 50,000 people showed up to witness the execution of de Roux and Manning.

A man who killed people to sell their bodies for dissection wound up dissected himself.

With his partner in crime William Hare, William Burke killed sixteen people, virtually at random, throughout 1828. Each time they killed they would sell the bodies to Robert Knox, a doctor and researcher, who would dissect the cadavers in medical lectures. After he was executed for his crimes, Burke became one of those dissected bodies.

Body parts from an unidentified murder victim were found by the home of the *Frankenstein* author.

The left half of a female torso surfaced in London's Thames River in September 1873. In subsequent days, the right half, some of the lungs, a thigh, a shoulder, a foot, and an arm emerged, and then a scalp connected to a face. A skull never materialized, so police tried to reshape the face over a butcher block and put it on public display for identification. One man thought it might be his daughter, but he wasn't sure. One other part of the victim was discovered thrown onto the property belonging to Mary Shelley, the deceased author of body parts–oriented novel *Frankenstein*.

Historically, lesser crimes were punishable by death.

In seventeenth-century England, many crimes other than murder could result in a culprit receiving a death sentence. One of those was "strong evidence of malice in a child." If a court proved that a kid was evil, or that they lacked the ability to know the difference between right and wrong, it could execute him or her. The malice charge was levied against many children aged twelve to eighteen who were put to death, but the youngest was John Dean, who, at eight years old in 1629, was executed for arson.

Breaking exile could get a person killed by the state.

Another crime that could lead to a death sentence in England a few hundred years ago: breaking exile and returning home to England. Beginning in the reign of King George I in the early 1700s, criminals were sent away in lieu of prison to Africa, Australia, or the Americas for a period of seven years, fourteen years, or life. If they ever came back, they'd be killed.

A French village truly believed that a werewolf was killing its children.

In the late sixteenth century, children started to disappear near the French village of Dole. Sometimes their mangled body parts would show up on the outskirts of town, leading local officials to believe the murderer was a werewolf. When citizens went out to hunt it, a search party found Gilles Garnier standing over a dead child. Garnier confessed to the murder and cannibalism of four children. He also admitted to the werewolf part, claiming a demon had given him an ointment that made him a bloodthirsty werewolf.

A Korean prince got away with countless murders, until he attacked a sibling.

Sado, the crown prince of Korea, brought terror to the royal court and palace in the 1760s. He'd rape women and kill random visitors and workers often and over a period of years, with contemporary accounts recalling multiple dead bodies hauled out of the palace daily. When he started to routinely attack his younger sister, his father, King Yongjo, delivered a punishment: He locked Sado inside a wooden rice chest. Eight days later, he'd starved to death.

A jealous john killed a prostitute and attributed it to sleepwalking.

Albert Tirrell ventured into a Boston brothel one evening in October 1845 to see his favorite working girl, Maria Ann Bickford. But when he arrived, Bickford was preoccupied with another client, and that threw Bickford into a jealous rage. He took it out on the woman and the rest of the staff. He cut her throat, killing her, and then individually set fire to three rooms in the brothel. A year later, a jury found Tirrell not guilty of murder, his lawyers arguing, without proof, that their client was a chronic sleepwalker who had committed his crimes while asleep.

CHAPTER 10

Various Charges, Crimes, and Offenses

The true crime genre is vast
and includes more than just murder
and serial killing. There are many
fascinating and gut-wrenching stories
involving kidnapping, robberies,
arson, corruption, financial
malfeasance, and organized crime.

Time is of the essence in kidnapping cases.

When a child is missing, authorities say that the first three hours are the most important, and if the abductee isn't found in that time, the odds of their safe return home are slim. About 76 percent of kidnapped children who are later found murdered were killed within three hours of their abduction. However, 99 percent of all kidnapped children do get home safely.

Missing kids have appeared on milk cartons since the 1970s.

The idea of placing photos of missing children on milk cartons began in Iowa in the mid-1970s. It became a national campaign in 1984, when the National Center for Missing and Exploited Children was established and used milk cartons to raise public awareness of kidnapped or missing kids. The organization was launched in the wake of the 1979 kidnapping of six-year-old Etan Patz, who never got on his school bus in Lower Manhattan. (His remains were never found. He was declared dead in 2001 when Pedro Hernandez confessed. Hernandez was sentenced to twenty-five years in prison in 2017.)

Amber Hagerman inspired the AMBER Alert.

AMBER Alerts are automatically pushed to phones in a city, state, or region when a child goes missing. AMBER is an acronym that stands for "America's Missing: Broadcast Emergency Response." The program was also named for nine-year-old Amber Hagerman. In 1996, while she was riding her bicycle in her neighborhood in Arlington, Texas, she was abducted and murdered.

A woman in Philadelphia started a house fire to cover up the kidnapping of a baby.

A fire broke out in the Philadelphia home of Luz Cuevas in December 1997. She attempted to rescue her ten-day-old baby daughter, Delimar, from her crib, but she wasn't there. Cuevas rushed out of the house with her other children, saving them and herself. Authorities later ruled that the baby must have died in the fire, caused by a faulty extension cord. Six years later, Cuevas attended a birthday party and saw a child who looked like her other kids and would've been the same age as Delimar. She managed to grab a strand of the girl's hair, and she persuaded police to open an investigation and test the hair's DNA. It was confirmed the child was Delimar. A cousin of her father, Carolyn Correa, had started the fire as a ruse to kidnap the baby.

Steven Stayner rescued himself and another kidnapped boy.

In 1972, seven-year-old Steven Stayner was kidnapped by sex offender Kenneth Parnell near Stayner's home in Merced, California. Parnell raised Stayner as his son Dennis (while also regularly assaulting him), and convinced the boy that his parents had turned over custody to him. At age fourteen, when he was tasked with recruiting Timmy White into his kidnapper's ring of torment, Stayner engineered his escape along with White's.

Tragedy continued to follow a boy who beat the odds by escaping his kidnapper.

After Steven Stayner escaped from sex offender Kenneth Parnell, his life and his family continued to be hindered by tragedy. Stayner died in a motorcycle accident ten years after his escape, and fourteen-year-old Timmy White, whom he'd saved from his kidnapper, served as a pallbearer. White would go on to become a deputy in the Los Angeles County Sheriff's Department, but he would also die early, at age thirty-five of a pulmonary embolism. A decade after Stayner's death, brother Cary Stayner committed four murders, for which he was later convicted and sentenced to death.

Police returned a kidnapped boy to his mother, except that he wasn't the right kid.

Nine-year-old Walter Collins set out from his home in Los Angeles in 1928 to go to a movie, and he never returned. More than six months later, Illinois State Police picked up a runaway, who told police he was Walter Collins. He returned home to his mother, Christine, and lived with her for three weeks. But Christine knew this wasn't her son—he was shorter, their dental records didn't match, and their behaviors were different. The police insisted the kid was the real Walter, because they wanted the case closed.

The mother of a returned kidnapped boy was sent to a mental institution when she attested that he wasn't her son.

The LAPD had Christine Collins committed to a mental institution for refusing to accept a twelve-year-old runaway named Arthur Hutchins as her missing son, even though she was right: He was not her child. The twelve year old eventually came clean and admitted he wasn't Walter Collins. Christine Collins was released from the psych ward and sued the LAPD, but she never found her child.

Frank Sinatra developed a lifelong habit after the abduction of his son.

In 1963, nineteen-year-old celebrity scion Frank Sinatra Jr. was kidnapped from his hotel room in Lake Tahoe. Three men were captured and imprisoned for the crime; the teen was safely returned two days after his abduction because his famous father paid a $240,000 ransom. All communications were conducted over pay phones, and calls cost ten cents at the time, resulting in a lifelong anxiety for the elder Frank Sinatra. Until he died in 1998, he always made sure to have ten dimes in his pocket.

A woman discovered that the person she thought was her mother was really her abductor.

In 2005, Connecticut woman Nejdra Nance became pregnant, and in order to apply for state-funded prenatal care, she needed her birth certificate. She asked her mother for a copy, and her mother put her off, finally claiming that she didn't have one because she'd unofficially adopted her as an infant from a drug dealer. Nance later went through missing persons files, found her own baby picture, and solved her own kidnapping. The woman who had raised her had swiped her from a hospital in 1987.

A child was taken from his uncle and sent to another family because authorities insisted that he was a kidnapped child.

During a family vacation to Louisiana's Swayze Lake in 1912, four-year-old Bobby Dunbar vanished. A massive search party formed, and the swamp was scoured, alligators examined, and part of the resort torn up to look for Dunbar's remains, but to no avail. Eight months later, Dunbar's uncle spotted the boy in Mississippi, found in the company of a homeless vagabond named William Cantwell Winters. Both the man and the child said the kid wasn't Dunbar, and that he was the nephew of his traveling companion. Nevertheless, the child was sent back to Dunbar's mother, where he lived out his days. Decades later, DNA testing proved the boy wasn't Bobby Dunbar.

The richest man in the world refused to pay the ransom for the return of his grandson.

John Paul Getty III was the grandson of oil tycoon J. Paul Getty, the richest man on the planet at the time. Living in Rome in 1973, sixteen-year-old Getty III was kidnapped by members of an organized crime family, who demanded a ransom of $17 million. The elder Getty refused to pay, and showing they meant business, the kidnappers followed through on their threat and cut off Getty III's ear. An eventual negotiated ransom of $3 million was paid to secure the teenager's release.

Patricia Hearst was kidnapped by community-minded radicals.

Patricia "Patty" Hearst, heiress to the vast Hearst publishing fortune, was kidnapped and held for ransom in 1974. But this case differed from other abductions of the wealthy's offspring. Hearst was gone for nineteen months with her captors. They called themselves the Symbionese Liberation Army, robbing banks to fuel their causes, and their ransom was the demand for all the poor and needy to be fed.

Patty Hearst participated in criminal activities with her captors.

Less than two weeks after her disappearance, Patty Hearst appeared in security footage of one of the Symbionese Liberation Army's armed bank robberies, brandishing a handheld automatic weapon. After her capture and return, Heart was prosecuted and convicted on bank robbery charges, despite a Stockholm syndrome defense, arguing that she'd been brainwashed and came to rely on and agree with her captors. In 1976, Hearst was sentenced to thirty-five years in prison, later reduced to seven, and then shortened by President Jimmy Carter and eventually pardoned by President Bill Clinton.

Elizabeth Smart's kidnapping went unreported for hours because the sole witness was terrified.

Fourteen-year-old Elizabeth Smart was kidnapped out of her bedroom in her family's Salt Lake City home in 2002. She shared a room with her nine-year-old sister, Mary Katherine, who fearfully pretended to be asleep when the abductors arrived. She ran to tell her parents what had happened after she thought the kidnapper had left, only to almost encounter him and Elizabeth in the hallway. So, she went back to bed for a few hours and then told her parents and reported details to the police, as she was the crime's only witness.

A prominent New Yorker didn't report his daughter's kidnapping because he didn't want the negative attention.

Socialite Dorothy Arnold, daughter of wealthy perfume importer Francis Rose Arnold, left her Manhattan home on December 12, 1910, to buy a dress. She stopped at a grocery store and bookstore, saw a friend, and didn't make her scheduled lunch appointment with her mother. She was never seen again, and it's possible police could have followed up had her father reported that his daughter was missing. He hired private investigators, because he didn't want the bad publicity, only filing a missing persons report a month later.

Ariel Castro kidnapped, and then held prisoner, a friend of his daughter.

Ariel Castro kept numerous women captive in his basement for a decade, routinely torturing and raping them. The youngest victim was teenager Gina DeJesus, a friend of his daughter, Arlene. He kidnapped her in 2004 after offering to drive her home from school. After her disappearance, he attended rallies and vigils to find Gina.

Gangster Al Capone fed the hungry people of Chicago.

Before President Franklin Roosevelt's New Deal set up a number of public relief agencies and a social safety net, charity was handled privately by churches and organized crime syndicates. In 1930, as a way of garnering favor with the public that would allow him to operate his criminal enterprise with little resistance, Al Capone fed five thousand hungry Chicagoans on Thanksgiving. In future years, he'd buy and distribute thousands of turkeys, purchased from small, locally owned grocery stores.

Al Capone got his nickname, and huge scar, while working as a teenage bartender.

Early twentieth-century Chicago gangster Al Capone was also known by the nickname "Scarface" because of some large, thin blemishes across his face. While tending bar at a gang-run New York City brothel as a teenager in the 1900s, Capone started a fight with a man by making rude comments about the woman he'd entered with—his sister. The individual attacked Capone with a knife, slashing him across the face.

Chicago's airport is named for the son of an underworld lawyer.

Mob lawyer Eddie O'Hare aligned himself with Al Capone's Chicago-based criminal organization and made a lot of money in the underworld when he teamed up with his boss to convert a dog track into Sportsman's Park, a major horse racing venue. Then O'Hare turned snitch, giving the IRS the info it needed to send Capone to prison, not for his violent crimes but for tax evasion. In November 1939, O'Hare was found murdered in his car; his son, Butch, a Navy flying ace during World War II, died a war hero in 1943. Chicago's O'Hare Airport is named for him.

A Mob informant died while under heavy guard.

Murder Incorporated, a consortium of multiple Italian and Jewish organized crime operations, employed Abe "Kid Twist" Reles until he turned informant for the New York district attorney's office in 1940. He delivered testimony for two full weeks, providing critical and damning details of dozens of violent crimes. As a result of Reles's reporting, four gangsters met their end in the electric chair. Carefully watched by law enforcement after his snitching, Reles somehow was pushed out of a window of his cop-guarded hotel room.

A brothel owner told the FBI where to find (and kill) gangster John Dillinger.

Born in Romania, Ana Cumpanas came to the U.S. in the 1910s and by the 1930s was running a brothel in Gary, Indiana, under the name Anna Sage. When caught for her illegal activities, she faced deportation but got out of it by offering the FBI assistance in catching Chicago gangster John Dillinger. Known as "the Lady in Red," she told authorities that she'd be attending a movie at Chicago's Biograph Theater with her date, Dillinger, and that she'd be wearing a crimson dress. Agents shot and killed Dillinger just after the film ended.

Virginia Hill was a muse and mistress for major Mafia figures.

Virginia Hill was romantically linked to several criminal underworld figures of the early twentieth century, including Frank Nitti, Frank Costello, and Joe Adonis. The so-called Mistress of the Mob was the star witness at congressional anti–organized crime hearings in 1951. She once claimed that Bugsy Siegel was a great love of her life, but she happened to be gone from her home the night rival gangsters killed him in her living room.

Richard Kuklinski is probably the most sadistic Mob enforcer in history.

Contract killing is generally thought of as a cold and efficient practice, but not for Richard Kuklinski, who seemed to take extreme sadistic pleasure in how he killed. He creatively murdered more than two hundred people as a freelance hit man for almost every major Mafia family active in the United States in the twentieth century. One such target endured Kuklinski cutting off his testicles, skinning him, pouring salt onto his flesh, and then feeding him to sharks. And on multiple occasions, he fed his victims to rats.

The head of New York's vice squad helped mobsters operate casinos.

Herman "Beansy" Rosenthal ran an illegal casino in New York City in 1912, and when he got busted, he told vice cops that he had an accomplice and co-owner: Lieutenant Charles Becker, head of the vice squad. It turns out that instead of busting casinos and brothels, Becker extorted their operators, demanding large cash sums to look the other way. After a few hours of questioning, Rosenthal was released and shot and killed on the street that day. The assailants were arrested, and they said Lieutenant Becker ordered the death. In an internal investigation, it was found that he'd taken more than $100,000 in extortion money in his nine months as head of vice. In 1915, Becker became the first American police officer executed for murder.

A serial arsonist took his cues from a finger tingle.

Peter Dinsdale was born to a British prostitute and grew up with disabilities. At age nineteen, he changed his name to that of his hero, Bruce Lee. He became a pyromaniac, acting when his fingers started tingling. He committed his first act at age nine, using his repeated pattern of sticking paraffin through a mail slot, then throwing in a lit match. He killed twenty-six people in this way.

A burglar caught in the act exposed the involvement of the Chicago P.D. in a crime ring.

Richie Morrison was picked up in July 1959 in the middle of burglarizing a Chicago store. And then he started talking, earning the nickname "the Babbling Burglar." Morrison admitted that he'd committed a slew of burglaries over the past fifteen months, all with the knowledge, help, and planning of eight Chicago police officers working the nightshift at the Summerdale precinct. They'd even escorted away the stolen money and goods with their squad cars. All eight officers were arrested and punished, and Chicago established a pioneering police board, a civilian panel that provides oversight to area law enforcement.

A huckster really did fraudulently sell and resell the deed to the Brooklyn Bridge.

The old scam about being sold the Brooklyn Bridge is based on one man's scheming. In the late nineteenth and early twentieth centuries, George C. Parker made a fortune by convincing wealthy but gullible tourists that major New York City landmarks were for sale, and that he could sell their ownership deeds. He variously sold off the Metropolitan Museum of Art, the Statue of Liberty, and the Brooklyn Bridge, which he sold at a rate of twice a week for thirty years. Arrested for his crimes in 1908, he escaped jail by putting on a stolen sheriff's jacket and hat, and he resumed his scams until 1928.

Criminals emptied an armored truck full of diamonds while the driver took a nap.

While on the way to the International Gem and Jewelry Show in Los Angeles in July 2022, the driver of an armed, secure Brink's security truck stopped at a Flying J Travel Center in Lebec. The driver took a nap and slept through a heist in which criminals emptied the truck of its valuable wares: twenty-two bags of gems, diamonds, and gold belonging to thirteen jewelers. It took them just twenty-seven minutes.

A German man's plan to scam Nestlé involved poisoned chocolate and carrier pigeons.

In the late 1990s, German Alexandru Nemeth attempted to blackmail the international food company Nestlé by inserting poison into some of its well-known chocolate bar products, then threatened to distribute them to the public, where they could kill innocents. In exchange for not releasing the deadly candy, Nemeth demanded diamonds from Nestlé executives. He sent his ransom notes via carrier pigeon, and requested they use the same birds to send him his gems. Police simply captured the birds and followed them to Nemeth's hideout.

A small-town doctor operated a lucrative baby-selling operation.

Dr. Thomas Hicks worked as the town doctor in McCaysville, Georgia, in the 1950s and 1960s, advertising abortions. He'd also encourage women to carry their children to term, telling them their babies died, then sell the newborns off the books to couples out of state for $1,000. This wasn't uncovered until 1997, twenty-five years after Hicks's death.

Authorities can now unblur photos and pull fingerprints from objects in pictures.

After arresting a man in 2012 for possession of child pornography, Danish police needed to nab the person who made the material, finding one clue as to their identity in the background of one of the photos in question: a pill bottle with a name too blurry to read. Police consulted with the U.S. Homeland Security department's Cyber Crimes Center, which used cutting-edge tech to unblur the name, obtaining parts of a name, medication, and prescription number. They were also able to obtain a fingerprint left on an object in the photo, tracing it all to one Stephen Keating, who got a 110-year prison sentence.

Two fake cops executed the biggest art heist in history.

Just before 1 A.M. on March 18, 1990, a fire alarm went off on the third floor of the Isabella Stewart Gardner Museum in Boston, home to one of the most illustrious and valuable fine art collections in the U.S. Security guard Richard Abath went to check it out, but he found no fire. Half an hour later, two Boston police officers buzzed into Abath's security desk, claiming to respond to a disturbance call. Abath let them in, and the cops said they recognized him from an outstanding warrant, taking him away from the desk and the silent alarm button. The other guard was taken aside, too, but only to be told by the fake police officers, "Gentlemen, this is a robbery." Both guards were duct taped to a pipe in the museum basement. Within ninety minutes, the robbers made off with thirteen works of art worth $500 million.

Two photos vanished from the Museum of Modern Art, and then just as mysteriously returned.

Two framed photos on display in the permanent exhibit of the Museum of Modern Art in New York disappeared without a trace in 2017. With a combined value of $105,000, it was a big loss for the museum. But four days later, they were returned, unaltered and undamaged. No witnesses to the crime ever transpired, nor was there any security footage or evidence. They simply disappeared and then came back.

A civil rights crusader robbed jewelry stores to fund his cause.

In 1963, Eddie Sandifer, living in Mississippi, a battleground in the civil rights movement, wanted to financially support the push for equality. So to generate funds, the nursing-home worker became a jewelry thief. He robbed six jewelry stores in all, timing the getaway from one so that he crossed train tracks right when a train was coming to cut off the police in pursuit. Sandifer was caught selling his jewelry at a pawnshop, and he did sixteen months in prison.

Three of the most notorious twentieth-century terrorists were all held in the same prison at the same time.

Ted Kaczynski (a.k.a. the Unabomber), Timothy McVeigh (the Oklahoma City Federal Building bomber), and Ramzi Yousef (who bombed the World Trade Center in 1993) all served part of their prison sentences at the Florence ADX "Supermax" facility in Colorado. Each was held in solitary confinement twenty-three hours per day but would often spend their one hour of shared recreation time together, and they became friends. They talked about old movies they liked.

A burglar accidentally became a deadly arsonist.

Peter Leonard had only meant to start a small fire in a closed bowling alley in Port Chester, New York, in 1974 to serve as a distraction while he robbed the place. The fire quickly got out of his control and rapidly spread to the adjoining Gulliver's Nightclub. Tried and convicted on many counts of murder, Leonard had his verdict overturned when a judge learned that police had abused Leonard in custody, with the charges reduced to reckless manslaughter.

A heroic California fire captain was actually a serial arsonist.

In the 1980s, John Orr served as the captain of the Glendale Fire Department in California, a job he earned in part due to his preternatural ability to show up to fight fires before anybody else on the force. It turns out that Orr was able to get to the scene so quickly because he was usually already there—he started more than two thousand fires from 1984 to 1991 that caused millions of dollars in property damage and the deaths of four people.

Fire captain and serial arsonist John Orr wrote a novel about a fire captain who is a serial arsonist.

Improved fingerprint gathering and identification technology in the early 1990s are what finally brought John Orr down, linking him to countless fires he started. Another piece of damning evidence in the trial of the serial arsonist who admitted to deriving sexual gratification from starting fires: Orr wrote a novel called *Points of Origin*, the story of a fire department official who is secretly an arsonist who gets thrills from fire.

A hunger strike staged in protest of an allegedly wrongful arson charge left a man's heart fatally inflamed.

James Richard Finch and John Andrew Stuart were held jointly, criminally liable for the arson attack that destroyed the Whiskey Au Go Go nightclub—and claimed fifteen lives—in Brisbane, Australia, in March 1973. Both attested to their innocence even after receiving long prison terms. Stuart was especially keen on proving he didn't do it, attempting to garner attention to his plight by staging a six-day hunger strike. That act inflamed his heart, and it killed him.

Every possible way to get a family out of their home in a 1945 fire was curiously, suddenly unavailable to them.

On Christmas Eve 1945, the Fayetteville, West Virginia, home of the Sodder family caught fire in the middle of the night. Parents George and Jennie Sodder, and four of their nine children, quickly and safely escaped. George Sodder went back in to head upstairs and rescue the others, but the staircase was impassable. Then he noticed his ladder was missing, and the truck he planned to stand on wouldn't start. One of the kids ran to a neighbor's house to call the fire department, and they didn't pick up.

The remains of some of the Sodder children supposedly lost in that fire never materialized.

The neighbor of the Sodder family drove to town, found the fire chief, and told him in person. Still, firefighters didn't arrive until 8 A.M., by which time the house had burned down. Authorities then went through the ashes to find the remains of the deceased Sodder children—but couldn't find them. The fire chief suggested the fire was so hot it cremated the children, but that wouldn't have happened in a house fire. The Sodders became convinced that their children had been kidnapped and the fire was a front, and they kept a billboard offering a reward for information up until 1989.

The Son of Sam was an arsonist as well as a murderer.

David Berkowitz, the Son of Sam serial killer who terrified New York City in the late 1970s, was also a serial arsonist, and a remarkably prolific one at that. After he was arrested and linked to murders, NYPD investigators found Berkowitz's highly detailed personal log of 1,411 fires he'd started, ranging from trash-can fires to vacant lots to abandoned buildings. Some were in close geographic proximity to the sites of Berkowitz's murders.

An angry unemployed man started a deadly fire after being thrown out of a nightclub.

After losing his job at a factory in the Bronx in 1990, a frustrated and angry Julio Gonzalez tried to blow off some steam at the Happy Land nightclub. While there, he got into a disagreement with his girlfriend, the club's coat check attendant, leading the bouncer to throw him out. Gonzalez then set the place on fire. Only six of the ninety-three people inside survived the arson, to which Gonzalez later confessed.

Teenagers in Sweden started a deadly nightclub fire because the cover charge was too high.

After four teenagers—Shoresh Kaveh, Housein Arsani, Mohammad Mohammadamini, and Meysam Mohammadyeh—argued with a bouncer over the admission price to a youth club in Gothenburg, Sweden, in 1998, they retaliated by dumping gasoline on an emergency stairwell and setting it on fire. It spread to the club, and with the emergency exit aflame, few could safely emerge. A total of sixty-three people died, and two hundred people were badly burned.

A crime writer got her ideas from her romantic relationships with murderers.

True-crime author Sondra London conducted her research in a most nontraditional but immersive manner. Her old boyfriend, G. J. Schaefer, committed a murder, and her later fiancé, Danny Rolling, was a serial killer. She pulled from her experiences with and observations of the two men to write psychological profiles of serial killers.